SACKED?

MADE REDUNDANT?

Your rights if you lose your job

A handbook for applicants to Industrial Tribunals

by Chapeltown Citizens Advice Bureau
   Tribunal Assistance unit
   cartoons by Harry Hamill

National Association
of Citizens Advice bureaux 1981

ISBN 0 906072 02 6

© NACAB 1981

Production by
Raven Oak Press Ltd.,
London, W3 8AW

TO OUR READERS

This handbook covers the whole process of going to an Industrial Tribunal about unfair dismissal or redundancy in detail. But you don't have to read all the handbook to get what help you need. The basic steps are easy: if you simply want to know these just read the bold type. The handbook is set out so that each section is as self-contained as possible, so you can go straight to the part you are interested in after a look at the Contents page. We have used cross-references a lot, and we hope the layout is easy to follow. Remember, the amount of detail you want to go into is up to you.

ACKNOWLEDGEMENTS

We wish to thank the Rowntree Charitable Trust for the initial funding to start this project, and the National Association of Citizens Advice Bureaux for the funding to see it to completion.

We received countless suggestions on the draft of this handbook, which have filled gaps in our knowledge and (hopefully) made it easier to understand. We want to thank everyone who made suggestions and comments, and in particular Rex Bird, Chris Carstairs, Gary Dore, Peter Farmeary, Ian MacDonald, Mrs P. Matthews, Ed Myers, Beryl Orchard, John Paysner, Danny Phillips, Jennifer Pitkin, Gwynneth Pitt, Alan Robinson, Howard Saunders, and Maureen Taylor. Forms in this handbook are reproduced by permission of the Controller of Her Majesty's Stationery Office.

Special thanks to Roger Bronkhurst LLB, Solicitor, hon. legal adviser to Hackney Citizens' Rights Group, to Dave Cutler of NACAB, and especially to Harehills & Chapeltown Law Centre.

Gordon Crawford, Will Iles, Hugo Storey.
Tribunal Assistance Unit, Chapeltown Citizens Advice Bureau.

NOTE

There are frequent changes in employment law. In particular, changes in regulations and new case law come up regularly. This handbook is as accurate as we have been able to make it on going to press, but we advise you to check elsewhere (see page 102) for recent changes.

List of abbreviations and key words

ACAS — Advisory, Conciliation and Arbitration Service - see page 73.

additional award — Part of the compensation an IT can award for unfair dismissal; given where a tribunal order is not followed - see page 155.

All ER — All England Law Report - see page 102.

applicant — The proper word for someone who makes a claim to an IT.

application — The proper word for a written claim to an IT.

associated employer — A company owned by your employer, or jointly owned with your company (ie both are subsidiaries of another company).

basic award — Part of the compensation an IT can award for unfair dismissal — see page 62.

CA — Court of Appeal.

CAB — Citizens Advice Bureau.

COIT — Central Office of Industrial Tribunals. Address in Appendix A

compensatory award — Part of the compensation an IT can award for unfair dismissal — see page 65.

constructive dismissal — Dismissal where your boss's conduct entitles you to leave but consider yourself sacked, so you can still claim unfair dismissal or redundancy page — see page 34.

continuous employment — Working out your period of "continuous employment" is essential to find out if you qualify to apply to the IT. For unfair dismissal and redundancy payment, a week counts towards continuous employment if you worked for 16 or more hours. There are 3 exceptions (schedule 13 EPCA):
a) If you work between 8 and 16 hours, this counts so long as it is for not more than 26 weeks, and you normally work more than this.
b) If you work between 8 and 16 hours, this counts if you have done this for at least 5 years.
c) Holidays, sickness, lay-offs, maternity leave, etc. also count.

CRE	Commission for Racial Equality. Set up by the Race Relations Act 1976. May help with an application about race discrimination in employment (as well as other fields).
cross-examination	When someone who has given evidence is questioned by the other side — so as to try to bring up points in the questioner's favour.
DE	Department of Employment.
DHSS	Department of Health and Social Security.
dismissal	For circumstances when you can consider yourself dismissed, see page 33.
EA	Employment Act 1980.
EAT	Employment Appeal Tribunal. Any higher appeal from an IT goes to the EAT. See page 158.
EAT rules	Employment Appeal Tribunal Rules 1976, S.I 1976/322.
effective date of termination of employment	This date is the date you need to work out to see if you have worked long enough to be eligible to apply to the IT. If notice (or pay in lieu of notice) is given, it is the date when notice runs out. If instant dismissal by the employer, it is the date on which you stopped work. If a fixed term contract, it is the date the fixed term runs out. If dismissal is by notice during industrial action, it is the date notice was given. For unfair dismissal, written reasons for dismissal, or working out the basic award: if notice given by the employer is less than the legal minimum, it is the date the legal minimum notice would run out. (s.55(4) & (5), 62(4)(a), 153(1)EPCA).
EOC	Equal Opportunities Commission. Set up by the Sex Discrimination Act 1975. May help with an application about sex discrimination in employment (as well as other fields).
EPA	Employment Protection Act 1975.
EPCA	Employment Protection (Consolidation) Act 1978.
evidence in chief	When someone gives their own evidence about the points they think are important, before they are cross-examined (see above) on it. It arises when there is no representative.
examination in chief	When a representative questions her own client, before the client is cross-examined (see above). It arises when there is a representative.
further particulars	More details of your case or your employer's case - see page 91.

HMSO	Her Majesty's Stationery Office.
ICR	Industrial Court/cases Reports — see page 102.
insolvency	Your employer is insolvent if he goes bankrupt, or if the company is wound up, or a receiver appointed (s.127 EPCA).
IRLR	Industrial Relations Law Reports — see page 102
IT	Industrial Tribunal.
ITEW Regs	Industrial Tribunal (England and Wales) Regulations 1965, S.I. 1965/1101.
ITR	Industrial Tribunal Reports — see page 102
ITRP Regs	Industrial Tribunal (Rules of Procedure) Regulations 1980, S.I. 1980/884.
IT1	Form for starting an application to the Industrial Tribunal — see page 48.
IT3	Form the employer uses to reply to the IT1 — see page 88.
LAG	Legal Action Group. Concerned with improving legal services and the law.
mitigation of loss	Means showing you have tried to reduce your losses caused by dismissal; eg tried the grievance procedure, looked for other jobs — see page 144.
NIRC	National Industrial Relations Court. This court no longer exists, but some decisions it made are still valid in law.
pay in lieu of notice	Pay given instead of notice when you are dismissed.
prescribed element	Part of the compensation awarded by the IT, from which any social security benefits you have received can be recouped by the DE/DHSS — see page 146.
recoupment	Recovery from your employer by the DE/DHSS of social security benefits you received — see page 66.
re-engagement	After dismissal you are taken on again by your old boss or an associated employer, but not necessarily in the same job or with the same terms — see page 50.
re-examination	When someone has given evidence in chief and been cross-examined (see above) is questioned by someone on their own side, so as to try to clear up points which came up in the cross-examination.

reinstatement	After dismissal you are taken on again by your old employer just as if you had never been sacked — see page 50.
respondent	The proper word for the "other side" in an IT case. Generally this is your own employer.
ROIT	Regional Office of the Industrial Tribunals. Addresses in Appendix A.
RPA	Redundancy Payments Act 1965.
RRA	Race Relations Act 1976.
s.	section
SDA	Sex Discrimination Act 1975.
statutory	Written in an Act or Regulation made by Parliament.
TUC	Trades Union Congress.
TULRA	Trade Union and Labour Relations Act 1974.
WLR	Weekly Law Reports — see page 102.

CONTENTS

How to Use this Handbook

Purpose Of This Handbook

Applications to Industrial Tribunals are now very common. There are about 35,000 applications a year, and in 1980 about 29,000 of them (83%) were claims of unfair dismissal. **There is a long list of complaints to do with your employment which you can take to an Industrial Tribunal — see page 5. Our aim is to assist everyone who wants to know about going to an IT with an unfair dismissal or redundancy case, from deciding if you are eligible to apply (appeal), through dealing with your employer and ACAS and preparing your case, up to the hearing and after. We give some practical guidance on each complaint, but this handbook only goes into a lot of detail about applications to do with unfair dismissal and redundancy.** Redundancy applications are likely to become much more common as the economic recession bites harder. This handbook should be very useful for other applications too, as much of the practical guidance applies generally to IT cases.

This handbook is different to others in that it emphasises how to deal with these problems in a practical, detailed and easy to understand way, from the worker's point of view. Our section on the hearing itself is less detailed because we don't think we can teach you to be a television lawyer. We think the best way to approach the hearing is with a well-prepared case. We hope you will find the handbook useful, whether you are applying on your own or assisting someone else with an application.

'If I'd known that protesting about getting the sack would cause this much trouble I'd have gone to an Industrial Tribunal instead

Even if you are eligible to apply, we want to stress that this may not be the first thing you should think of doing. If you can get what you want at work through your trade union taking action or, if you are not a trade union member, through a direct approach to management, so much the better. The legal right to go to an Industrial Tribunal is a valuable one, but it isn't a substitute for negotiation or industrial action. Disputes about almost all employment rights lead to an IT. These rights are *individual* rights, whereas traditionally the exercise of workers' rights has rested in *collective* strength. There may be a conflict between the rights of an individual and the rights of the workforce. Indeed, it is an open question whether ITs have any useful role. As well as undermining the collective struggles, IT applications are now much harder to win than they used to be. Favourable decisions have decreased steadily from about 40% in 1975 to 28% in 1978.

If you are not eligible to apply to an IT, page 8 and Table 2, page 182, tell you what paths are open to you.

Our Audience

This handbook is written for people without legal training. We hope it will be useful both to people helping workers with a case, such as trade unionists and advice centre workers, and to workers who are applying on their own. This handbook is written to assist employees and their helpers. Employers may find some of the information useful, but should consult a CAB or the Small Firms Information Service.

We hope this handbook will encourage and help trade unionists and other lay advisers to get involved in preparation of and assistance with applicants' cases at ITs. By lay advisers we do not just mean paid workers but also voluntary workers in CAB and other advice centres. People applying to ITs have few sources of advice to turn to. Many applications are withdrawn because of fear or non-preparation, or lost through lack of preparation, or settled at a figure way below entitlement. Help from a trade unionist or adviser, even with limited time and experience, can be vital. If you are a shop steward or works convenor, consider helping with the case yourself rather than passing it on to a district official. Discuss with the district office how feasible this is. Aside from the help you can give, it can also be an effective way of understanding useful employment law.

The preparation stages of an IT case are well suited to an adviser's or trade unionist's role; interviewing, negotiation by phone, form-filling and letter writing. Final preparation involves access to case law, but this can be overcome by using the trade union district office, or a solicitor through the Green Form scheme (see page 22), or by consulting a local law centre or Tribunal Assistance Unit.

Should you be a helper or a representative? (helpers and representatives only) Quick method

At the hearing itself, we don't necessarily expect volunteers or trade unionists to be representatives. Tribunals expect representatives to be skilled in cross examination and legal argument, and to follow procedure and formality properly. Usually they will not assist a representative in putting her case, although they may give some help to a representative without legal training. Although many advisers and trade unionists can become competent representatives, an alternative and extremely good way of helping the applicant at the hearing is not as a representative, but rather as an *assistant.*From now on we refer to anyone who takes on this assisting role as the "helper". The applicant can conduct her own case at the hearing, with the helper sitting next to her taking notes and offering advice. Less preparation time is involved, and the tribunal will be less formal and more ready to assist the applicant present her case. The section "The Hearing" lays particular emphasis on this 'assisting role'.

Many advisers and trade unionists can and do represent fully at ITs, however, and if you feel you can meet the demands, we would certainly not wish to discourage you. If you decide to represent, don't hesitate to tell the Chairperson that your experience is limited, as the tribunal will probably allow for this. If you are representing, the section "The Hearing" will give you most of the information you need, but you may also want to look at "The Industrial Tribunals Handbook" (see Appendix B), which goes into legal procedures in more detail. The decision whether to be a helper or a full representative will also depend a lot on the applicant's ability to conduct her own case. If she is not able to express herself well, for example, it would be best to represent her.

How To Use This Handbook

This handbook starts with sections on what's involved in applying to an IT, and then goes through the process for unfair dismissal from the earliest stages onwards. Because not everyone using this guide will want to read the whole of it, we have designed it so that each section stands on its own as much as possible. So if you prefer, you can simply turn

4

to the section dealing with the stage which concerns you. For example, if you have just heard from ACAS, you can turn to "Negotiation", page 73. **There is a special section at the end on redundancy and insolvency cases.** These are becoming more common with the growing economic recession, so we have gone into the issues in some detail.

Quick method

For a quick method of reading through sections, read only the sub-headings and the lines in heavy black type, like these. This is also the method to use if you want to know the basic essential steps but not the details.

Abbreviations and strange words

You enter a special world of strange words when you bring a case to an IT. Instead of making an 'appeal', for example, you are "the applicant", who makes "an application" to the IT. Your employer becomes "the respondent". If you do not understand the meaning of any abbreviation or strange word, look it up in the list on page ii.

What Else You Need To Know

If you have an unfair dismissal or redundancy case, this handbook should tell you most of what you need to know. If you are taking a different complaint to the IT, there are wider legal areas which are not covered here. In either case, you will probably want to look at:

"Rights at work"

"Rights at Work" by Jeremy McMullen. This is an excellent, easy to read (but not too comprehensive) book for workers on how to use the law on the whole range of individual and trade union rights, especially if you are applying about something other than unfair dismissal. See Appendix B, no. 1.

Other books and leaflets you might want to use are:

Background information

1. The Department of Employment (DE) "Employment Protection" series of 14 pamphlets. They give useful information on redundancy, maternity rights, medical suspension, union rights, guarantee payments, unfair dismissal, and employment protection generally. There are also codes on picketing and the closed shop. There is a full list in Appendix B. You can get them, free, from any DE office.

2. The Advisory, Conciliation and Arbitration Service (ACAS) "code of practice" leaflets on how bosses and workers should behave. They are 15p each from HMSO, and listed in full in Appendix B.

Case law

It will often help to look at other books as well – particularly those giving previous similar cases to compare to yours. The decisions which have been reached in the previous cases are important because on matters of law they will strongly influence the tribunal when they decide your case (see page 102). This 'case law' is found in more specialised books and journals, which you should find in the reference section of big libraries. If you are unable to get them or find them too complicated, don't worry. Perhaps an advisor, trade union district office or solicitor (see page 22) can sort out the case law for you. If not, go ahead with your case anyway – the tribunal should sort out case law at the hearing.
3. The "Encyclopedia of Labour Relations Law" by Hepple and O'Higgins, or "Harvey on Employment Law" both contain all the law and case law up to a certain date, and are brought up to date periodically.
4. "Industrial Relations Law Reports" is a monthly journal which reports recent cases, and is fairly easy to use. Other journals also give recent case law and changes in law.
5. IDS 'Handbooks', 'Supplements' and 'Briefs'. The handbooks cover the whole range of employment topics through relevent law and case law, and are easy to read and follow. The supplements and briefs (only available to subscribers), update the handbooks and provide a really comprehensive guide. They go to all IT members, too.

All these books and journals, plus other useful books, handbooks and reference works are listed in Appendix B.

Other actions

If, besides going to an IT, you are taking some other action against your boss (suing him in the County Court for failing to give you holiday pay you are entitled to, for example), you may well need advice about this – see page 22.

1. WHAT YOU CAN APPLY ABOUT

What You Can Apply About

There is a whole range of matters about which you have a right to apply to an Industrial Tribunal. Each subject has different conditions attached to it — eg,- time limits for applying. Table 1 pages 9-16 sets out each subject and its conditions, and the IT can give you if you win.

*Note.*This table is not in legal language and is a general guide to individual rights only. For the exact legal language and rights of trade unions look at the law, Hepple and O'Higgins, or Harvey (Appendix B pages 16 and 18.

Powers Of The IT

ITs have wide powers which include orders for reinstatement, as well as financial compensation. Their exact powers depend on what you apply to them about (see Table 1). Note that the awards listed in the table are the *maximum* awards.In many cases they may give you a lot less (see page 19). This is particularly true in discrimination cases, where the compensation if you win is often less than £100.

'Personally I like your 'Industrial Tribunal' idea, but I don't think THEY'LL buy it'

Is It Best To Apply To An IT?

Involve your trade union

Your case may be one that could go to an IT, but this many not always be the best thing to do. You should first consider:

1. Union action, or action by your workmates, on your behalf. The law is not designed to meet workers' needs, many workers are not covered by its provisions, and tribunal members can be out of touch and unsympathetic. Direct action can be both a lot more effective and quicker in getting what you want, and it can help other workers with similar problems later on. Other courses open to you are banning overtime, working to rule, occupying, striking, etc. If the problem is a common one affecting a number of people then these should be the first things you think of. Whether you choose one of these courses is up to you, and only you on the spot can decide the pros and cons. Go through your union and try and get union support for your action. If there is no union, think about joining one. Your union representative should also activate the firm's grievance procedure (see 2. below) and any other procedures for reconciliation.

Follow the grievance procedure

2. **Your firm's "grievance procedure"** (the established way for sorting out problems between workers and employers). Look in your contract of employment to see

8

TABLE 1

SUBJECT	TIME LIMIT FOR APPLYING (these are not always absolute – see page 26).
1. Any dismissal. Your right to ask for written reasons as to why you were sacked. The reasons must be true and in reasonable detail. Your boss has 14 days to give the reasons. You can apply if he unreasonably refuses. (s.53 EPCA).	Within 3 months of being sacked (s.53(5) EPCA).
2. Unfair dismissal. Your right not be sacked or made redundant unfairly. Pages 33 and 169 go into this in more detail. (s.54EPCA, ACAS code of practice "Disciplinary Practice and Procedures in Employment").	Within 3 months of the "effective date of termination of employment" – see page ii (s.67(2) EPCA).
3. Redundancy and insolvency. a) Your right to a redundancy payment and a written explanation of how it's worked out (s.81, 91, 102 EPCA).	Within 6 months of leaving (s. 101 EPCA).
b) Your right to an insolvency payment from the Secretary of State when your boss goes bust. (s. 124 EPCA).	Within 3 months of the Secretary of State's decision (s.124 EPCA)

9

APPLICATIONS TO INDUSTRIAL TRIBUNALS

CONDITIONS	POWERS OF THE I.T. (the maximum amounts are revised each year).
You need to have worked continuously for 26 weeks. Otherwise see 2. below (s. 53(2) EPCA).	2 weeks gross pay. Declaration of the real reasons why you were dismissed.
You have been dismissed (see page 33). You are under 60 (women) or 65 (men) or the normal retirement age for your grade (s. 64(1) EPCA). You have worked continuously for at least 52 weeks (s.64(1), 151(2) EPCA). You are not self-employed, employed by your wife or husband (s. 146(1) EPCA), or by a foreign government, or a share fisherman (s. 144 (2) EPCA, policeperson (s. 146(2) EPCA), docker (s. 145(2) EPCA), or someone who normally works abroad. You are not employed by a small firm (less than 20 employees) which sacked you within 2 years of starting there (s. 64A EPCA, s. 8EA). See 10. below if you were sacked for trade union membership or activities.	Up to £16,910 compensation, reinstatement or re-engagement (basic, compensatory and additional awards — see page 62).
You have been made redundant and have not unreasonably refused an offer of alternative work. You are older than 20 and younger than 60 (women) or 65 (men). You have worked continuously for your employer for at least 2 years. You are not self-employed, a docker, a share fisherman, a merchant seaman, someone who normally works abroad, a home help employed by a close relation, or employed by your wife or husband, by the Crown, or by a foreign government. Some health service and oil rig workers are also excluded. (s.81(1)&(4),82(1), 151(2),145(3),144(2),141(4),100(2),146(1),99,137, schedule 4 para 2, and schedule 5 EPCA).	Up to £3,900 redundancy payment.
You have applied to the Secretary of State for an insolvency payment for certain debts under s. 122 or 123 EPCA.	Declaration of the amount that the Secretary should pay.

c) Your right to have time off work, with pay, to look for a new job or retraining (s. 31 EPCA).	Within 3 months of the day on which you wanted time off (s.31(7) EPCA).
d) Your right not to be chosen for redundancy unfairly — because of your trade union activities; or established procedure not followed in your case; or there was no consultation (where there is a trade union); or your boss didn't look for alternative work for you; or your boss didn't give you enough information about the alternative work for you to decide properly whether to take it. (s. 59 EPCA, s.99 EPA, Industrial Relations code of practice p.46, EAT decisions). This is one way of being unfairly dismissed — see 2. above.	See 2. above or 10 below.

4. Discrimination.

a) Sex discrimination. Your right not to be discriminated against because of your sex or because you are married (SDA).	Within 3 months of the event you are complaining about. If the EOC or CRE brings the complaint, within 6 months. If the EOC act for you and a non-discrimination notice has been given, within 5 years. (s. 62,68 RRA, s. 71,76 SDA).
b) Race discrimination. Your right not to be discriminated against because of your colour, race, nationality, ethnic origins (eg gypsies), or national origins (RRA).	

5. Maternity.

a) Your right not to be sacked because you are or have been pregnant, and to be given suitable alternative work if you can't do your own and a vacancy exists (s. 33,60 EPCA).	Within 3 months of the effective date of termination of employment (see page ii).

As 3a) above, except health service and Crown workers and people employed by a foreign government also have this right, but merchant seamen do not (s. 144(4) EPCA).	Up to 2 days pay.
See 2. above or 10. below.	Up to £16,910 compensation, reinstatement or re-engagement (basic, compensatory and additional awards – see page 62).
You are working, looking for work, or have been sacked or refused promotion. You do not work in a private household. If you are a partner in a business, there are at least 6 of you. For sex discrimination only, you are not in the armed forces, or the clergy, or a midwife, and if you work in a small firm there must be at least 6 workers. (s.6,11,19,20,85 SDA, s. 4,10 RRA). There are **no** conditions about age, how long you have worked, etc. You can claim unfair dismissal **as well as** discrimination if you meet the conditions of 2. above.	Up to £6,250 compensation. A declaration of your rights. A 'recommendation' to your boss to take some action.
a): You have worked continuously for at least 52 weeks. You are not in one of the excluded jobs listed in 2. above. (s.64(1),151(2)EPCA).	a) and b): Up to £16,910 compensation, reinstatement or re-engagement (basic, compensatory and additional awards – see page 62).

b) Your right to return to work at any time within 29 weeks of the birth, and to claim unfair dismissal or redundancy pay if refused (s. 33,45,47,56 EPCA).	Within 3 months of the day you said you would return. If you were sacked or made redundant before fixing a date, within 3 months of leaving (s.67(2) EPCA).
c) Your right to maternity pay from your boss whether or not you return to work afterwards. (Note. You may also be entitled to a National Insurance maternity allowance and/or grant). (s.33(1),34 EPCA).	Within 3 months of the last date on which you should have been paid (s. 36(2) EPCA)
d) Your right not to be unreasonably refused paid time off for ante-natal care (s. 13(6) EA).	Within 3 months of the day of the appointment (s. 13(7) EA).
6. **Equal Pay.** Your right to equal pay with a man (or woman) who does or did a basically similar job (the legal wording is more detailed than this).	While working, or within 6 months of leaving (s.2(4) EPA)
7. **Pay statement.** Your right to have an itemised pay statement each time you are paid. (s.8 EPCA).	While working, or within 3 months of leaving (s. 11(9) EPCA).
8. **Contract.** Your right to have a correct written statement of the particulars of your employment, and of any changes in them (s.1,4 EPCA).	While working, or within 3 months of leaving (s. 11(9) EPCA).

b) and c): You have worked continuously for 2 years by the time of the 11th week before the week your baby is expected to be born begins. You are still 'employed' at the end of the 10th week – this does not mean that you actually have to be working, just that your contract still applies. You have told your boss in writing that you are going to be away because of your pregnancy, and that you intend to return to work, at least 3 weeks before leaving. 3 weeks before you return, tell your boss in writing. (Your boss is not obliged to take you back in the same job if it is not "reasonably practicable" to do so and if you refuse suitable alternative work. And your boss is not obliged to take you back if there were less than 6 workers in the whole undertaking when you left and it is not "reasonably practicable" to take you back). (s.33(3),47(1),56,151(2) EPCA, s.11,12 EA).	c): 90% of 6 weeks pay, less flat rate maternity allowance (whether actually claimed or not).
You provide, if asked, a doctor's, widwife's, or health visitor's certificate that you are pregnant and an appointment card or other evidence to the appointment has been made (not required for your first visit). (s.13(2) & (3)EA).	Declaration that you were unreasonably refused time off: payment of the money you should have received (s.13(8) EA).
There must be a man (or woman) who you can compare yourself with through a job evaluation study. The man must work (or have worked) for your boss or an associated boss. He must work (or have worked) at your "establishment" or at one with the same terms and conditions. (s.1 EPA).	Declaration that you are entitled to equal pay, and up to 2 years arrears of pay (s.2 EPA)
You are not a merchant seaman or a share fisherman. You work continuously. (s.144(2)&(4),151(2) EPCA).	Declaration of how your pay is calculated. Up to 13 weeks arrears of deductions you haven't been told of (s.11(8) EPCA).
You must have worked for 13 weeks. You are not employed by the Crown, a docker, or working normally abroad. You are not employed by your husband or wife. (s.1(1),138(1),141(1),145(1),146 (1) EPCA).	Correct statement (s.11(5)& (6)&(7) EPCA).

9. Guarantee payments. Your right to a 'guarantee payment' if your boss suspends you or lays you off for a day or more. (This applies if your contract allows your boss to do this without your agreement. If not in your contract, you may be able to claim unfair dismissal, redundancy pay and breach of contract (s.12 EPCA).	Within 3 months of the day for which you are claiming (s.17 (2) EPCA).
10. Trade union membership and activities. a) Unfair victimisation. Your right not to be victimised for trying to become, or being, a member of an independent trade union, or for carrying out union activities (s.23 EPCA).	Within 3 months of the victimisation (s.24 EPCA).
b) Unfair dismissal. Your right not to be sacked for trying to become, or being, a member of an independent trade union, or for carrying out union activities (s.58 EPCA).	Within 3 months of the effective date of termination (see page ii), or 7 days if you use 'interim relief' procedure to stop a sacking (s.67(2),77(2) EPCA).
c) Time off for activities/duties. Your right to have time off for union activities or duties (s.27,28 EPCA, Health & Safety at Work Act 1974, ACAS code of practice 3).	Within 3 months of the day your boss refused you time off (s.30(1) EPCA).
d) Your right not to be unreasonably refused membership of a trade union, or unreasonably expelled from a trade union (s.4(4)EA).	Within 6 months of the date of refusal of membership or expulsion. If the application for membership is ignored, the date is the end of the period in which you could reasonably expect an application to be dealt with. (s.4(6) &(9) EA).
e) Your right to compensation from the trade union once d) (above) has been declared (s.5(1)&(2) EA).	At least 4 weeks after the declaration date, and within 6 months of the declaration date (s.5(3) EA).

You must have worked continuously for at least 4 weeks. You have not been hired on a fixed term contract of 12 weeks or less. You have not been hired for a job which is expected to last 12 weeks or less. You are not employed by your wife or husband. You are not a share fisherman, a docker, or someone who normally works abroad. You are not in the armed forces or the police. (s.138(3), 141(2),143(1)&(3)&(4),144(2),146(1)&(2) EPCA).	Up to £8.75 per day you have been laid off. Limit of 5 days per 3 month period. (s.15(1), 17(3) EPCA).
You are not a share fisherman or someone who normally works abroad (s.141(2),144(2) EPCA).	Declaration of your rights. Compensation (not limited). (s.24 EPCA).
As above.	Up to £16,910 compensation, reinstatement or re-engagement (basic, compensatory and additional awards – see page 62). Under "interim relief", an order for your contract to continue, reinstatement or re-engagement.
You are a member or an official of an independent trade union **recognised** by your employer (s.27(7) 28(4) EPCA).	Compensation (not limited) (s.30(2)&(3) EPCA).
No conditions.	Declaration that you have been unreasonably refused membership or expelled (s.4 (7) EA).
No conditions.	Up to £16,910 compensation (s.5(7)&(8) EA).

what it is, or ask your shop steward. Every firm except small ones should have one, even if it's not written down. Take your problem as high as possible within the firm – right to top management if necessary. Always try and have someone with you when you meet management, either your shop steward or other union representative, or a workmate if you're not unionised. If management insist on you alone, it's best still to see them. Even after you're sacked it may be worth seeing management. For example, if you were sacked in the heat of the moment after a row with the foreman about safety procedure, it may be possible to get your job back straightaway. Or there may be an internal appeal you can make through the firm's disciplinary procedure.

Make sure management know all the facts. You may not have deserved sacking but if management did not know facts in your favour they may still have been acting reasonably in sacking you.

The grievance procedure is very important. Even if it seems a waste of time, it should be tried. The fact that you have tried will be a point in your favour at any future IT. And if you didn't try to follow the grievance procedure, it can be a point against you.

Negotiate

3. **Negotiation.** Even before you apply to the IT, it may be worth trying for a settlement if you have a strong case. You could contact your employer directly, or ask ACAS to mediate between you. Your chances of getting your job back are highest at this early stage, before your boss gets a solicitor and starts on the road towards a tribunal hearing. Point out to your boss that taking you back now would save all the cost of hiring a solicitor (assuming he is not a member of an employers' association, or would represent himself).

Note for helpers

If you are an advice centre helper, would it help at this stage to ring up: 1) the union representative or district office 2) if no union or it is not feasible, the firm and see if any conciliation is possible? Consider asking ACAS to intervene if there seems a possibility of settling the problem without applying to an IT.

Watch the time limit

One important thing to remember if you are not applying straightaway — watch out for the time limit for applying. For unfair dismissal, this is 3 months. **If the time limit is coming up, put your application in anyway: you can withdraw it later if your problem is solved in another way.**

Are There Other Things You Should Be Claiming?

As well as, or instead of applying ot an Industrial Tribunal, there may be other matters you want to take up elsewhere — in the County Court, for example. Table 2 on page 182 lists some of the most common.

2. WHY APPLY?

Here is a very brief outline of what happens when you apply to an IT about unfair dismissal. This is all covered in much more detail later in this handbook.

What Happens When You Apply?

1. **You fill in an application form claiming unfair dismissal.** This starts the official machinery for informing your employer and heading towards a hearing.

2. **After about 2-5 weeks you get a copy of a form your boss filled in giving his case,** but often in very little detail.

3. **ACAS should contact you and your employer to see if there is any possibility of settling your claim without going to the tribunal.** If there is a possibility, ACAS will be there as a go-between right up to the hearing.

4. **You have the chance to ask your boss for more details of his case, and to get them ordered** if he will not **supply them.** This is called getting "further particulars". **You can also order witnesses to attend the hearing.** (You can get the hearing postponed if you have a good reason. The tribunals are often strict about this once the hearing dates have been agreed).

5. **There is a possibility at this stage of a "preliminary hearing", or alternatively a "pre-hearing assessment"** if you or your boss request it or the tribunal Chairperson suggests it.

6. The actual hearing usually takes place about 8-10 weeks after you applied. Your employer (or his representative) and you (or your representative) both put your cases to the tribunal. The tribunal normally tell you their decision at the end of the hearing. If you win you will probably get compensation or your job back.
7. There is a possibility of further appeal, but only on a point of law.

Is It Worth Applying?

If you think you have been sacked unfairly and meet the conditions listed in Table 1 then it may be worth applying to an IT. But, as we said on page 2, this should be the second thing you think of, not the first. If your union or workmates will take action for you to get your job back, this may be a much more sure and better way than going to an IT. If a tribunal finds you have been unfairly dismissed it is more likely to award you compensation than order that you should get your job back.

The maximum compensation possible is at present £16,910 — there are yearly increases (this made up of a basic award of £3,900, a compensatory award of £6,250 and an additional award of £6,760: see page 61). The amount actually awarded can be surprisingly low, however — the majority get less than £400.

Figures for 1977 and 1978 on applications to ITs about unfair dismissal show that just over a third of cases are settled before the hearing, usually with a sum of money being paid to the applicant. Of cases which go on to the hearing, just over a quarter are won by the applicant (figures from "Employment Gazette", May '78 and Sept. '79).

What if it's a weak case

If you're sure you have a poor case, then obviously it's better not to apply. But if in doubt, apply. There is little chance of a tribunal ordering you to pay your boss's costs if you lose, although this is becoming more common. The tribunal can **only** do so if it thinks you acted "frivolously or vexatiously or otherwise unreasonably". That is, just to get back at your boss and not because you thought you had a case; or if you postponed the hearing or fail to turn up without good

19

reason (usually if you have caused your boss unnecessary expense). Bringing your case or conducting it "unreasonably" was introduced in October 1980 (rule 11(1) ITRP Regs). Obviously many cases which are neither frivolous nor vexatious could be considered to be unreasonably brought or conducted. Also see page 146. The IT should not make you pay costs just because your case *turned out* to be hopeless. The possibility of costs can cause a great deal of worry. They are far removed from the intention of ITs to be "informal and inexpensive". The increasing possibility of costs can only put off applicants applying to ITs even though they believe they have real grievances — this is most unsatisfactory.

What if you don't have help

Getting involved in an application on your own can be a big step into the unknown. Don't take it lightly — it can be a hassle. But we hope this handbook will give you confidence to take this step. We believe most people can do it, either on their own or with help.

See below for details of people and organisations that might be able to help you with your application.

3. HELP WITH AN APPLICATION

Do You Need Help?

You can apply and win without help from anyone. Many people who apply do it without help, and without representation at the tribunal. (In 1979, 50% of people applying were represented, compared to 65% of employers). The basic steps of the process are simple, and you can use this handbook to help you.

But it does help to get advice and possibly assistance from others, especially those experienced in this area. It can boost your confidence and improve your chances of success. It can give you an idea of what sort of case you've got — whether strong or weak, whether you should pursue it or withdraw it. Help can be given at different stages of the process — not just at the tribunal hearing. This is particularly important with ITs, because familiarity with legal questions can be an asset, or things may in fact be quite complex. As it may not be possible to get someone to represent you at the hearing, try to get advice as soon as possible after your dismissal.

Getting help does not have to mean handing over your case completely. Assistance up to the hearing can be a joint effort between you and your helper. But if you name someone as your "representative", the Industrial Tribunals office will deal only with that person — you will have to make sure you keep in touch. And at the hearing your representative will take the main part — you will only be able to speak in reply to questions. (This contrasts greatly with appeals to other tribunals. We think it bad that applicants should be kept so removed from the events that effect them so much).

Some helping organisations may only be willing to help you up to the hearing itself;others will also assist or represent you at the hearing.Some may only assist on a joint basis,either on principle or because they can only help in a limited way.Some help all comers,others only if they think your case is a good one.

Who Can Help?

Many different groups and individuals help with applications: below is a list of those which may be able to help.
Trade Unions (see note below)
Citizens Advice Bureaux
Commission for Racial Equality (CRE)
Equal Opportunities Commission (EOC)
Free Representation Units (often attached to a university or polytechnic law departments)
Law Centres
Solicitors (see note below)
Tribunal Assistance Units/Tribunal Representation Units

Note on trade unions

Trade unions are a very common and often the best source of help with applications to ITs. About 16% of applicants are represented at tribunal hearings by trade unions. Trade unions often employ people whose only job is to assist with applications to Industrial Tribunals and similar employment matters (suing bosses

21

for compensation, for example). Their representatives are usually very experienced and knowledgeable, although they are sometimes too busy to devote a lot of time to preparation of a case. If you are a trade union member, we would always recommend you contact your shop steward or union district office about your case. The union's help is free, and covers all aspects of an application, including representation. If you aren't a union member, join a union so you can get help from it next time.

Note on solicitors

If you are considering a solicitor's help, the question of payment will come up. You may be able to get free, or reduced cost help under the "Green Form" legal assistance scheme (up to a limit of £40, or about 2 hours work) if your income is low enough. Solicitors can apply for an extension to the scheme for more than £40, but you may need to ask them to do this. The Green Form scheme covers preparation for the hearing (for example help in writing for "further particulars", or checking case law). *It does not cover representation at the hearing, The cost of representation could be around £200 per day.* One possiblity, however, is that the solicitor could come to the hearing to *advise* rather than to represent, and then claim for this through Green Form scheme extension.One problem with the Green Form scheme is that if you win,your solicitor may claim back some of the money from you.Another is that some solicitors refuse to do *any* IT work under the scheme.

Section 2 of the Legal Aid Act 1979 clears the way for regulations to allow solicitors to represent at IT hearings under the Green Form scheme extension. Unfortunately there are no immediate plans for such regulations to be brought in.

We would advise you to consider a solicitor's help only if you know of one experienced in, or keen to learn about, employment and IT work. A local CAB, advice centre, or law centre could probably suggest one. Alternatively, a good advice worker may know as much and be able to put in more time on your case than a solicitor.

Starting a Case

1. INTRODUCTION

The range of issues and complaints you can apply about to an Industrial Tribunal has already been listed (Table 1, page 9). We aim to give some guidance on all these matters, but only deal in detail with the most common, unfair dismissal and redundancy. About 83% of all applications to ITs were for unfair dismissal in 1980.

This section covers what you have to check and find out before filling in your application form. Some of the things you'll need to think about are:

*are you eligible to apply?
*are you within the time limit?
*what are the good and bad points of your case?
*is action needed on other problems?

If possible, consider these with a helper or representative.

2. BEING A HELPER/
REPRESENTATIVE

Referral to union   First ask about the date of dismissal. It's very easy to
miss a time limit and there may be insufficient time to
contact a trade union. Then ask the applicant is she is a
union member. If yes, you should normally refer her to
her union official. It may be best to approach the shop
steward, branch secretary, or works convenor first if
one of them is likely to give active help. Union officials
are best contacted at the District Office of the union.
It's a good idea to ring up the official, make an appointment for the applicant, and discuss the case with the
official. If she is not a union member, or the union will
not help because, for example, she has not paid up her
subs, or she has not been a member long enough, then
it is up to you to help. (Advise her to pay her subs. up to
date before she goes to see the official). Referral to the
trade union may not always be possible.

   If the applicant does not want to approach the union
you have a problem. We suggest you contact the trade
union anyway — perhaps the problem can be sorted
out, or else the union could give you clearance to go
ahead and assist the applicant.

   At the hearing, if you are helping or representing a
trade union member, tribunal members, especially
trade union members, often view the absence of a trade
union representative with suspicion. If there was the
opportunity to allay such suspicion by explaining the
circumstances and policy (normally to refer union
members to the union and only to help subsequently if
there is a special difficulty about the union representing), all would be well. Unfortunately there is usually
no 'slot' at the hearing in which to raise this and suspicion often unfairly remains. Where you are helping
or representing a non-union employee, again trade
union tribunal members may be unsympathetic,
especially if there is a union in existence at the workplace. Try and explain the reasons why you are helping
or representing at the start of the hearing.

   If one of the original ideas of ITs was that tribunal
members should include people familiar with the
problems and viewpoints of both employer and employee, then it must be said that trade union members

do not necessarily always fulfill this role in relation to union members, let alone non-union applicants. We would hope for more understanding from them in relation to non-union lay representatives whose cases often fall into one of the above two categories. In particular we would like tribunals to bear in mind that lay agencies are usually representatives because there is no-one else to help.

Being a helper/ representative

How much you help with an IT application can vary a great deal. It depends on what the applicant wants and how much you are willing to do, and at what stage in the proceedings you become involved. It could take up quite a lot of time. But you and the applicant must sort this out at the start. Make it clear what degree of help you are prepared to give: whether you can only help with the application form; whether you will give help all the way through and assist or represent her at the hearing; or whether you will help her so far and refer her elsewhere for free representation.

Find out what the applicant wants. She may want a helper to do most things for her, or she may just want some advice and support in dealing with the application herself. This should prevent any misunderstanding about what she expects of you, and create mutual trust and confidence to approach the application together. We recommend that you act as a helper rather than a representative unless you are experienced or strongly wish to represent — see page 4.

Keeping in touch

Please note that if you are the named "representative" for an IT application then you and only you receive all the correspondence from the Tribunal Office and from the employer's representative. The applicant will not be sent anything. So remember to keep the applicant informed of developments, and send her copies of letters, etc. If you do not put yourself down as "representative", but are still helping, then it will be up to the applicant to keep in contact with you.

3. ELIGIBLE TO APPLY?

Eligibility Conditions

Imagine you have some trouble at work, like your boss has laid you off and refused you a guarantee payment. You have tried the grievance procedure (see page 8) without any result. Is the problem something you can apply to an IT about (see Table 1, pages 9-16)? Assuming it is, you must then **check whether you personally are eligible to apply. To be eligible you usually have to be over or under a certain age, and to have worked for a certain length of time. These conditions differ with each problem.** For some complaints, you can apply as soon as you start work, eg equal pay. With others, eg race or sex discrimination, you can apply without being in work if, say, you were refused a job and you think it's because you're female or black.

The sort of things you have to check are:
*How long you have worked and that this has been "continuous" (see page ii).
*The number of hours you work each week.
*Your age.
*That you are not one of the exceptions who cannot apply.

See Table 1, pages 9-16, for a full list of what you have to check for each problem.

If you are not sure whether you are eligible

If you are not sure whether you are eligible to apply, get advice. If still in doubt, *send in your application.* Eg you want to claim unfair dismissal, but you're not sure if you worked continuously for 52 weeks. Don't hesitate to apply. The employer's (respondent's) reply may clarify things or at least isolate the issues in dispute. The tribunal will probably have a "preliminary hearing" to decide if you are eligible or not — see page 112.

Time Limits

Late applications

You have to apply within a certain time. For example, for unfair dismissal, you must apply *within* 3 months of the date you finished work. See Table 1, pages 9-16, for a full list of time limits.

Note that your application must be *received* at the Central Office of Industrial Tribunals (COIT) by the time limit.

The IT can only allow late applications to be heard if it wasn't "reasonably practicable" for you to apply within the time limit (schedule 1, para. 21(4) TULRA). **In practice ITs are much stricter about time limits than**

most other tribunals. Only if you have very good reasons will they allow a late application, and then only if your late application was made in such further time as was reasonably practicable.

On October 6th 1976, R was sacked on suspicion of theft. She gave evidence that she had consulted the Citizens Advice Bureau about claiming unfair dismissal, and the bureau had wrongly told her they could not consider her claim until after her criminal case had been heard. On August 4th 1977, R was acquitted on the criminal charge, and on August 9th (8 months late) she presented a claim of unfair dismissal.

The CAB held that the tribunal could not hear her complaint. Where either an applicant or her advisers are ignorant or have a mistaken belief about the time limit, the tribunal must decide if the ignorance or mistake (whoever made it) is reasonable. If not (the applicant or adviser has an unreasonable belief or is at fault) then the claim could have been made in time. Here either R or the CAB had a mistaken belief which was unreasonable, and R's application was dismissed.

RILEY v TESCO STORES LTD and GREATER LONDON CAB SERVICE LTD. (1980)IRLR 103: CA.

Note: the CAB or any other adviser, even a volunteer, can be responsible for ensuring a claim is made in time. If it is not, the applicant could sue the adviser for failure to do this.

So make sure you don't miss the deadline. If you do, still send in your application if you have some really good reason for being late. The IT will probably have a "preliminary hearing" (see page 112) to decide whether to allow your application to be heard.

4. SIZING UP THE CASE

Assuming you've found out that you can apply to an IT, you must now start thinking about your case. Don't rush to fill in the application form (unless you are near the time limit deadline or wish to get your job back. Also remember that if you get a better paid job your compensation for loss of earnings will be getting less the longer you wait).

**Gathering
Information
questionnaire**

If you have a trade union or advice centre helper, both of you need to have a good chat about what happened. For unfair dismissal cases, use the questionaire on pages 29-32 to collect as much of the information you will need.

*Write down what
happened*

As soon as possible after your dismissal, write down in your own time and in your own words exactly what happened. This is often very useful both for your helper and for yourself. Give a full and detailed account. Write down the details of the incidents that led to your dismissal, eg the argument with the foreman about the safe way to move long metal girders on the fork lift truck. Try to give your account in chronological order, with dates and times if possible. Try to keep it as *factual* as possible—what you know happened, not your own opinion about what happened or what you heard only indirectly. Also write out the history of any previous complaints about you, your grievances, conflicts with management, etc. This is very important. You and your helper/representative must be clear about this as your employer will usually seek to exploit any blemish on your record. It may also help to write down a full description of your work and working environment, so your helper/representative understands the reality of your work situation. The tribunal may also find this useful.

28

Example of questionnaire to help gather useful information in unfair dismissal cases.

NAME OF APPLICANT   NAME OF RESPONDENT (employer)

ADDRESS   ADDRESS (give Head Office if known)

tel: tel:

Best times to ring:

....

....

1. What is your present age and date of birth?

2. Are you a trade union member? If so, which one? (Are you fully paid up? How long have you been a member?)

3. How many hours are you contracted to work? How many do you actually work?

4. Have you a written contract of employment? Have you seen it? Can you produce it? If not, have you anything written which refers to terms (eg in letter of acceptance)?.

5. State the address of the place where you worked, if different from that given at the start.

6. What was your job with these employers? Please give your clock number (if any).

7. What did your job involve? (Please give brief description).

8. State when your employment began with your ex-employer. If, during your employment, you had a number of jobs with *this* employer list all the jobs and give, if possible, the dates relating to change to different work. Has the firm changed hands?

9. Did you leave of your own accord?

10. Did any circumstances force you to leave? Did the employer's attitude/behaviour/conduct force you to leave? Give details.

11. Were you sacked? On what date exactly were you sacked? (ie the date when your notice ran out or, if you were dismissed without notice, the date on which you were told you were sacked).

12. If sacked with notice, how much? When does/did the notice expire?

13. Did you receive payment in lieu of notice? Is there any outstanding holiday pay?

14. If you were given a written notice of termination of employment please supply it.

15. Has your firm a grievance procedure? Please supply a copy if possible.

16. Has the procedure been followed? Have you refused to follow it? If so, please give reasons.

17. Is there an agreed disciplinary procedure? Produce a copy if possible.

18. Did anyone at your ex-employers interview you or anyone else or carry out an investigation into the circumstances?

19. Who dismissed you? Give his or her name and title at work.

20. Were you given an opportunity to explain yourself? If so, give details of how you were able to put your side of the case.

21. Who was present — shop steward, convenor, union official? Were they consulted before you were dismissed?

22. State, if known, why your employers will say they dismissed you.

23. Describe the events and circumstances leading up to your dismissal.

24. Do you agree that the reasons given by them are factually correct *but* do not give adequate or sufficient reason for dismissing you?

25. Do you disagree with the factual grounds given by them? In what ways?

26. Have you had any verbal warnings? Give details and dates if possible.

27. Have you had any written warnings? Produce if possible, otherwise give dates and details.

28. List the names and addresses of every person who can give evidence on your behalf, relating to the circumstances leading up to your dismissal, or your general conduct or ability.

29. If there have been similar circumstances to yours involving workmates who have not been dismissed, state what happened to them and give an account of the circumstances in those instances.

30. Has lack of skill or competance anything to do with your dismissal? Are there any works rules which apply in cases of lack of skill or competence? If so, please supply a copy. What training and supervision did you have in this job? Were you given an opportunity to improve with help and further training?

31. Has trade union membership, attempted membership, or representation anything to do with your dismissal? Give details.

32. Is your firm a closed shop and were you sacked for non-membership of a trade union?

33. What was your rate of pay with your ex-employers? Please give your weekly earnings including overtime and bonuses, before and after deductions.

34. List all payments received on termination of your employment, including holiday pay, pension payments or rights, and any redundancy pay.

35. Has any lump sum "ex-gratia" payment been made to you? How much and how was it calculated?

36. What is your National Insurance number and which office dealt with your claim for unemployment benefit. When did you sign on? If there was a delay, why was this?

37. Give the dates between which you were unemployed. If you are still unemployed, state what steps you have taken to find another job.

38. If you have found employment state the name and address of the new employers and the weekly amount of your earnings.

39. Have you lost any of the following as a result of your dismissal: pension rights? fringe benefits? free accomodation? use of a company car? luncheon vouchers? free transport? any other benefits? If so, please give details.

40. As a result of change of employment do you work longer hours/shorter hours/the same hours/unsocial shifts? Have you less responsibility/less skilled job?

41. Have you incurred expenses looking for jobs?

42. Have you asked for the reasons for dismissal in writing? When? Any witnesses?

43. Have you made any attempts to settle your claim? What was the result?

44. Have you already started proceedings? Have you filled in/sent off the IT1? Does the ACAS officer know? Who is representing/assisting you?
45. What kind of remedy do you seek? Reinstatement/Re-engagement/Compensation?

46. Is there any further information that you think may be useful?

5. INFORM ABOUT INDUSTRIAL TRIBUNALS

(for helpers/ representatives only)

When you first talk with someone about a possible IT case, remember she might not know much about ITs, and may well be nervous and worried about applying.

Discuss with her any worries she might have. Will she be put off or frightened by the formal nature of the proceedings? Might there be any adverse consequences? How long is the hearing likely to last? Is it like a court? Will there be publicity? Will it cost her anything? And so on.

6. APPLYING THE LAW TO YOUR CASE

The Law On Fair And Unfair Dismissal

The next thing is to apply the law to the information you've got, to see whether you have a case for redundancy pay, unfair dismissal, or whatever you are claiming. Can you fit you case into legal definitions? **Beware of forming a conclusion about the merit of your case here – your task is simply to see if you could benefit from the legal provisions relating to your particular claim.**

What follows is the law on fair and unfair dismissal, put into easy to understand English. Mr Justice Phillips said: "The expression 'unfair dismissal' is in no sense a common sense expression capable of being understood by the man in the street". Well, we'll do our best .....

You can find the law in:
* EPCA sections 54–80.
* SDA section 6(2).
* RRA section 4(2).
* You may also want to look at ACAS code of practice "Disciplinary Practice and Procedures in Employment".

What Counts As Dismissal?

The first big legal point is: was there a dismissal? You can only claim unfair dismissal if there has been a dismissal. Very often this is obvious and not disputed, but this isn't always the case. Some cases are largely about whether a dismissal took place or not. If you prove it did, it is more likely than not that your dismissal will be unfair.

You are dismissed if:

* Your boss sacks you, verbally or in writing, with or without notice. This can be explicit (eg "You're fired"), or implied (eg "We won't be needing you after the end of the month").

* Your boss refuses to renew a fixed-term contract.

* You leave during the period of notice of dismissal, provided you tell your boss before you leave (and, in redundancy payment cases, he doesn't object (s.85 EPCA)).

* Your boss refuses to re-employ you after a strike or lock-out.

* Your boss refuses to let you return to work after pregnancy.

* You are forced to leave due to the behaviour of your boss or his agent when your contract is breached by him in some important way. This is called "constructive dismissal" – see below.

Constructive dismissal

In many cases, workers are not directly sacked, but are forced to leave due to the boss:

– harassing a worker until she "leaves" or "resigns" (and so seems not to be dismissed).

– changing the job drastically, by altering what the worker does, her pay, hours, status or other conditions. (This is really sacking her from her job and taking her on in a new one).

'I think you could call this 'constructive dismissal' – but can they PROVE it!'

– suspending without pay, if not allowed for in the contract.

– behaving in such a way, even without necessarily meaning to, as to make it impossible for a worker to continue (eg sexual assault).

In these circumstances, a worker who leaves without being sacked can consider herself dismissed, and has the right to go to an IT to claim unfair dismissal (s.55(2)(c)EPCA). This sort of dismissal is called "constructive dismissal". Your boss's conduct entitles you to end the contract of employment and consider yourself dismissed.

If you go to an IT and claim constructive dismissal, *it is first up to YOU to prove that you were dismissed.* So when you fill in your application (see page 48) you have to give more detail than if your boss had simply dismissed you.

What you have to show at the hearing is that your boss's conduct showed that he did not intend to be bound by the contract of employment – that he *seriously* breached ("repudiated") the contract. This can be a breach of a written term in your contract or a breach of an implied term (eg your boss's duty to pay wages promptly, or to take care of your safety).

Following a five day disciplinary suspension without pay, S asked W to help him out of financial difficulties and when they refused he had to leave in order to get his holiday pay. S complained that he had been unfairly dismissed, and an IT found that he had been constructively dismissed.

The CA, allowing an appeal by W, held that constructive dismissal was not "unreasonable conduct" of the employer where the unreasonable conduct was not based on the contract of employment. *There must be a significant breach of contract by the employer going to the root of the contract, or conduct showing that the employer no longer intends to be bound by one or more of the essential terms of the contract. Furthermore, if the employee remains for any length of time following the conduct complained of, he will be treated as having affirmed the contract.* There· had been no breach or repudiation by W, so S was not constructively dismissed.

WESTERN EXCAVATING (ECC) LTD v SHARP. (1978)ICR 221; (1978)ITR 132; (1978)IRLR 27; (1978) 2 WLR 344: CA.

This is at present the most important case on this subject, and sets the standard for deciding whether a constructive dismissal has occured.

S, the manageress of an off-licence, worked overtime as agreed (a total of 88 hours) over Christmas. She was not paid any of this overtime, despite phone calls, until February 24th when she was paid for 40 of the hours. She then phoned head office, and the area secretary and the manager both told her that was all she was getting. Next she spoke to the assistant area manager who said he would sort it out for her and ring her back. S said if she did not get the money by the next day she would resign, and as she heard nothing further this is what she did, claiming unfair constructive dismissal.

The EAT, overturning an earlier IT decision, allowed S's appeal. The statements of the area secretary and manager were a breach of going to the root of the contract, and nothing that happened later affected this. Giving the employer only 1 day to pay was not unreasonable in the circumstances, and she had been constructively dismissed.

STOKES v HAMPSTEAD WINE CO. LTD. (1979)IRLR 298: EAT.

If you think your boss's conduct may force you to leave, remember to see your trade union representative first in case things can be sorted out. Send your boss letters of complaint. If you are forced to resign, point out in a letter to your employer that you consider he has repudiated the contract, giving your reasons for saying this. This is important, as otherwise constructive dismissal tends to be hard to prove. You will probably need to show:

a) a breach of an important part of the contract.
b) that this breach was why you left.
c) that you didn't act too soon, and
d) that you didn't delay too long.

What does not count as dismissal

You are NOT dismissed if:
* **You agree to leave your job** (but see "constructive dismissal", above). (You are dismissed if you are persuaded to resign to avoid being dismissed).
* **Your contract is "frustrated"** — this includes a worker's death, long illness, serious injury, imprisonment or a legal ban.

* **You were sacked while taking part in a strike or other industrial action, or during a lock-out** (s.62 EPCA), **UNLESS one or more also taking part were not sacked, OR one or more who also took part were re-engaged, while you were not.**

Automatically Unfair Dismissal

The second big legal point is: was it a dismissal which is automatically unfair? Your dismissal will automatically be regarded as unfair if you are sacked because of:
* **Trade union membership or activities** (s.58(1) EPCA).
* **Sex or race discrimination** (s.6(2) SDA, s.4(2) RRA).
* **Pregnancy** (s.34,60 EPCA).

Both of the first two reasons are often very difficult to prove.

In this sort of case, your job will be to show it was a dismissal principally for this reason, and your employer will be trying to show some other reason, eg not pregnancy but your bad work record.

Trade union membership and activities

1. *Trade union membership or activities.* This protects all members and people who try to become members of an independant trade union who are dismissed for a reason connected with their membership. This applies even if the union is not recognised by your boss (see POST OFFICE V UPW and CROUCH. (1974)ICR 378: House of Lords).

It is up to YOU to prove you have been dismissed for this reason, and applications are not often successful — tribunals are rarely prepared to say that an unfair dismissal was related to trade union membership.

If you are dismissed you can try the "interim relief" procedure (s.78 EPCA) to save your job. You need to act within 7 days of the dismissal. This leads quickly to a hearing in front of a tribunal chairperson, who can order your wages to be paid and job continue until there is a full hearing of the case. This claim is seperate from an unfair dismissal claim, though you can claim **both** at the same time.

Sex or race discrimination

2. *Sex or race discrimination.* You can complain *both* about unfair dismissal because of discrimination and about the discrimination itself. But showing

discrimination is the difficult part — there are few successful cases. You can get advice and sometimes help from the EOC or CRE in bringing your case — see Appendix A. Also see Appendix B, no. 11.

Pregnancy

3. *Pregnancy.* If you are sacked because you are pregnant, even though you are quite capable of carrying on at work, the sacking is automatically unfair.

If you are sacked for reasons *connected with* your pregnancy (eg you can't do heavy work, or your boss objects to time off attending the hospital), then your boss has to prove that you couldn't adequately do the work you were employed for, or it would break the law for you to carry on, AND that he offered you a suitable alternative job (if one existed). There is also a second hurdle for him — see page 39. Even if you are sacked for reasons connected with your pregnancy, and you lose your claim for unfair dismissal, you still keep your rights of maternity pay and to return to work if you would have had 2 years continuous service by the 11th week before the week you expect your baby.

'It seems a bit much losing my job at the pram factory for being pregnant'

38

Apprentices' rights Generally, it is more difficult to sack apprentices than other workers. However, the law and case law on dismissal for apprentices is not straightforward and you should consult a Tribunal Assistance Unit, law centre or solicitor (under the Green Form scheme) for advice.

Automatically fair A certificate signed by, or on behalf of, a Minister, saying that your dismissal was to safeguard national security, (eg in the nuclear power industry) will automatically make your dismissal fair (schedule 9, para 2 EPCA).

Reasons For Dismissal

Now we come to the third legal point. Helpers and representatives will have to get to grips with the technical words that come up here, in particular "substantial reason", and "acted reasonably". They are confusing at first, but are explained in what follows.

We assume there has been a dismissal, and the dismissal is not **automatically** unfair or fair (see above). **To defend the claim you have made, your boss now has 2 hurdles to jump:**

First hurdle: substantial reason for dismissal **1. Your employer has to fit his reason for dismissing you into one of a number of categories allowed by the EPCA. These reasons allowed by the Act are called "substantial reasons". They are:**
* **redundancy (s.57(2)(c) EPCA).**
* **incapability or lack of qualification (s.57(2)(a) EPCA)**
* **misconduct (s.57(2)(b) EPCA).**
* **closed shop (s.58(3), 58A EPCA, s.7EA).**
* **to employ you breaks the law (s.57(2)(d) EPCA).**
* **"some other substantial reason" (s.57(1)(b) EPCA).**

second hurdle: employer acted reasonably **If your boss shows a substantial reason allowed by the EPCA, then the tribunal has to decide whether he "acted reasonably" in treating the reason as "sufficient reason" to warrant sacking you, considering all the circumstances (s.57(3) EPCA).**

There are two aspects to this hurdle. First your boss has to show that the reason was serious enough to

merit sacking (a "sufficient reason"). For example, an employer might prove Shirley Jones was guilty of certain misconduct, but the IT might decide dismissal was unfair if she had not been given any warnings, or the opportunity to remedy her misconduct or improve her performance.

'Ignore it, it's just the boss trying the old harassment tactics on me again'

Second he has to show that the right procedure for dismissal was followed. Even if the employer shows serious misconduct, for example, he has also got to show that proper dismissal procedure (consultation, negotiation, appeals, etc.) was followed. **If you win a case on this point alone, then your award of compensation will always be reduced** (see page 64). In deciding this, the tribunal will consider the size of your firm. If you worked for a small firm and your boss did not follow proper disciplinary procedures, the tribunal will be more sympathetic to him than if you worked for a large one.

The substantial reasons of the first hurdle are very broad and often a boss is able to make out one of them as the reason for dismissal. But the second hurdle, whether your boss acted reasonably in sacking you for this reason, taking all the circumstances into consideration, can nearly always be challenged.

In more detail, the substantial reasons for dismissing you are:

Redundancy

1. *Redundancy*. See "Redundancy and Insolvency", page

Misconduct

2. *Misconduct*. This is a common reason, and covers many different actions. Some are:

* swearing. Often bad language is accepted by tribunals as commonplace on the shopfloor.

* fighting. Evidence of provocation, self-defence, etc. could be important.

* absenteeism and lateness. How much absenteeism or lateness is the important question.

* refusing to carry out an order, clocking someone else's card, etc.

If you stole from the till at work, or smashed up some of your boss's equipment, or refused to carry out some reasonable order after a period of "unsatisfactory conduct", your boss would probably call this "gross misconduct" and sack you without notice. But a single act of misconduct will often not justify instant dismissal.

If your boss can show misconduct, then he has jumped the first hurdle.

Mr A, who was working on nightshift, was dismissed after he had been caught sleeping in a "bed" when he had finished his quota for the shift. An IT held that he had been unfairly dismissed. No reasonable employer would consider that sleeping on nightshift after the worker had completed his work was an act of gross misconduct. Nor had Mr A been warned that this would be regarded as gross misconduct.

AYUB v VAUXHALL MOTORS LTD. (1978)IRLR 428: IT.

Mrs F was taken on as the full-time teacher in charge of the resources centre at a large comprehensive school. She was told that she was to work almost full-time at the centre and only to do sufficient classroom teaching to enable her to "keep in touch with practical requirements". Two years later F was asked to teach, and taught, 12 English lessons a week in addition to her work at the resources centre. When she was later told that she was now to teach 18 lessons a week she refused to do this, stating it would interfere with her work at the centre. She was dismissed and successfully claimed unfair dismissal. The IT held that she had acted reasonably in refusing to teach the extra lessons and was not guilty of misconduct. The EAT dismissed the employer's appeal and upheld the IT's decision.

REDBRIDGE LONDON BOROUGH COUNCIL v FISHMAN. (1978)ICR 569: EAT.

Incapability

3. *Incapability*. EPCA says this could be to do with your "skill, aptitude, health, physical or mental qualities". The most common sacking for incapability is when a worker is off sick or injured for a long time, or when it is thought someone is not doing the job well enough. So if your employer says you have been sick or injured for a long time, and can satisfy the tribunal that this was the reason for your dismissal, he has jumped the first hurdle.

D was ill for 5 months. His employer got a medical report, simply saying that D should be retired early on the grounds of ill-health, and as a result he was dismissed. He claimed unfair dismissal.

The EAT, upholding the IT's finding of unfair dismissal, said D should have been consulted and given an opportunity to state his case, and get independent medical advice.

EAST LINDSAY DISTRICT COUNCIL v DAUBNEY. (1977)IRLR 181:EAT.

Closed shop

4. *Closed shop.*. If you refuse to join the union, or leave the union, where there is a closed shop, then your dismissal will be for a substantial reason, and your boss has jumped the first hurdle. But there are many exceptions: if you genuinely object on the grounds of "conscience or other deeply held conviction" to joining the union; or if you were not a member of the union when the closed shop agreement was made; or if a closed shop agreement is made after the Employment Act 1980 came into force, and is not agreed to by at least 80% of those entitled to vote in a secret ballot; or if you are a member of another union which is involved in a recognition dispute with the closed shop union, and the dispute has been referred to ACAS, who are still considering the matter.

Breaking the law

5. *Breaking the law*. If continuing in your job would be breaking the law, either by you or by your employer,

your boss has a substantial reason for dismissing you. For example, if you were found to be a carrier of some disease, you could not continue to work in food processing.

P was employed as a trainee hearing-aid dispenser. The Hearing Aid Council Act 1968 provides that trainees must qualify within 5 years of their names being registered, unless the Hearing Aid Council have extended that period. P took 4 qualifying examinations and failed each year. His 5 years were due to expire the following month. The employers "genuinely took the view that he would never pass" and decided that rather than commit offences under the Act they would dismiss him. P successfully claimed he had been unfairly dismissed. The employers had not applied for an extension for P and had not warned him that he had better apply for one. The EAT observed that continuing in his job would not necessarily have involved breaking the law; they upheld the IT's decision.
SUTCLIFFE AND EATON LTD. v PINNEY. (1977)IRLR 349: EAT.

"Other substantial reason"   6. *"Other substantial reasons"*. This is included in the EPCA to cover other situations which may justify dismissal. It is up to the employer to state what the reason is and up to the tribunal to decide if it is a substantial reason or not (and up to you to dispute whether it is). **If an employer cannot base a dismissal on any of the other substantial reasons, "some other substantial reason" is generally successfully used to include it. Even if the employer does not include the dismissal in this category, the tribunal are likely to do this for him.** "Some other substantial reason", as interpreted, undermines the whole purpose of defining substantial reasons. **As a result, the first hurdle is usually a very easy one for the employer to jump.** Normally, therefore, it is not a good idea to base your case on disputing whether or not you have been dismissed for a substantial reason.

Two reasons often given in this category are "personality conflict" and, worryingly, where there is an important change in the worker's contract (without her agreement), but the change is necessary "in the interests of the business".

Miss T worked in an office. The atmosphere in the office had become so tense that it was unbearable and was seriously affecting the company's business. The cause of the trouble was a personality clash between Miss T and the other employees for which Miss T was to blame. Apparently the hostility arose "from a difference of opinion as to the merits of the permissive society" and Miss T "was completely insensitive to the atmosphere .... She already had an illegitimate child and now she was boasting of her association with a boy almost half her age". The IT held that this was "some other substantial reason" and the dismissal was not unfair.
TREGANOWAN v ROBERT KNEE & CO. LTD. (1975)IRLR 247: CA.

| Some Special Situations | In these situations, questions of fairness or unfairness are looked at in a particular way. There is a special burden on either the employer or the worker to prove sections of their case. |

Unfair selection for redundancy

1. Unfair selection for redundancy. See page 174 for details about this.

Temporary employees

2. Temporary employees. You are sacked and told that you were just a replacement for someone who has now come back to work. If you were not told of this in writing when you started, then claim unfair dismissal. Remember, you must have 52 weeks service.

Industrial disputes

3. Industrial disputes. Here the law is designed to prevent strikers from normally claiming unfair dismissal. If you are sacked during a strike or lock-out or any other industrial action, you may claim unfair dismissal if:

* one or more of the other workers involved in the dispute has not been sacked.
* one or more of the other workers involved in the dispute was sacked but then taken on again in the same job or in another similar job, and you were not offered your job back (s.62 EPCA).

The burden of the proof is on YOU in both these cases.

S, together with the vast majority of employees of J, went on strike to obtain the reinstatement of two colleagues dismissed for union activity. J gave notice that, unless the strikers returned to work on a certain date, they would be taken as having been dismissed. S was dismissed for not returning on the specified date. Prior to that date, two employees who had been on strike returned to work. The IT dismissed S's claim of unfair dismissal, holding that she had not shown that "one or more employees who also took part in the action were not dismissed for taking part in it"; although the two employees who had returned to work had not been dismissed they were not relevant since they were not on strike when S was dismissed.

The QBD, allowing an appeal by S, held that the tribunal was not justified in departing from the words of the law, read in an ordinary straightforward sense; the two employees who had returned to work were employees "who also took part in" the action and, as they had not been dismissed, S's dismissal was unfair.

STOCK v FRANK JONES (TIPTON) LTD. (1976)ICR 237; (1976)ITR 63: CA

*'Well, you can't say we were UNFAIRLY dismissed, at least NONE
of us got our jobs back after the strike!'*

Spent convictions

4. **Spent convictions.** If you are sacked because your firm finds out that you have a criminal record, then check at your local CAB, advice centre or trade union district office if this conviction is now "spent". "Spent" means that it no longer affects your job, etc., and you need not mention it to anyone. The Rehabilitation of Offenders Act 1974 s.4(3) says that a conviction is spent after a certain time, depending on the crime and the

sentence. For example, a sentence of 3 months in prison is spent after 7 years. So if your crime is spent, you should not be sacked for it. Claim unfair dismissal. But note there are a number of jobs this does not cover. Check that your job is not one of these.

Medical suspension 5. **Suspension on health and safety grounds.** This is called either "medical suspension" or "health and safety suspension". It happens only where workers in certain industries are exposed to certain harmful chemicals, dust or fumes. You may be sacked because it would be dangerous for your health to continue doing that job, as for example if a doctor reports you've gone over the "safe" (!) limit of exposure to radiation.

Don't worry too much about getting a bad dose here .....,
they usually sack you before that happens.

Or you may be sacked because your boss is aware of the dangers after a certain time and does not want to get stung for compensation. Check with your local Health and Safety Executive (see Appendix A) or Health and Safety Action Group to see if your job is one of those covered by the law (schedule 1, EPCA). If it is, you should *not* be sacked but suspended on full pay for up to 26 weeks. This applies only where you are capable of working, but where you should not be exposed any longer to the dangerous substance.

46

If your work involves chemicals, dust, fumes, etc., then contact the Health and Safety Executive and ask to be examined by one of their doctors from the Employment Medical Advisory Service. If you are over the "safe" limit, they will tell your boss. You should be suspended on full pay or offered different work. If sacked, claim unfair dismissal. To apply, you only need to have worked for 4 weeks, not 52 weeks (s.64(2)EPCA).

Summary

Remember — a substantial reason is not enough by itself for a tribunal to decide a dismissal was fair. The tribunal must also decide whether sacking the worker for that reason, rather than other disciplinary action, was reasonable, and if the manner of dismissal was reasonable. And in making those decisions the tribunal will examine all the surrounding facts. For example, if it would break the law to keep you in your job, a reasonable employer should look for ways of continuing employment without breaking the law, or see if there is an alternative job for you.

Note for helpers/ representatives

Be careful about advising people too hastily that they do or do not have a case for claiming unfair dismissal. A case may look weak to you on the immediate facts, eg Shirley Jones may admit her misconduct, but after examining all the circumstances and applying the law and case law, an IT may decide dismissal was unfair. However, if you are sure the person has no case you will need to explain why and encourage her to withdraw (see page 146).

7. THE IT1 APPLICATION FORM

Filling In The Form   So having checked your eligibility and thought about your case a bit, you have decided to apply to an IT. You may want to ask for written reasons for your dismissal before you apply (see page 55 - "Section 53 Claim") - *but watch the time limit.*

Here is some help on how to fill in the application form. This is known as the "IT1" form. You can get it from your local Job Centre, unemployment benefit office, or trade union, or perhaps CAB or advice centre. You should get a leaflet (ITL1) with the form. Fill in *two* copies of the form and keep one for yourself. There is an example of a completed IT1 form on pages 51-52.

Your own form   You don't have to use the official IT1 form to put in an application. If you can't get hold of one, or if the time limit for your application is nearly up, write out the following details:
* your name and address.
* the name and address of your employer.
* what you're applying about, eg unfair dismissal, plus brief grounds for your application (why you were dismissed and why you think it was unfair).
* sign and date it.
KEEP A PHOTOCOPY OR A CARBON COPY.

Some hints on   Here are some hints on filling in the IT1 form:
filling in the IT1   *Item 1.* Just put what your complaint is, eg unfair dismissal, or unfair redundancy, or redundancy payment, or unreasonable refusal to provide written reasons. Put down more than one complaint if relevant or if you're doubtful about which to claim. If you are putting in a written reasons claim together with another claim, see the special note "Section 53 claim" on page 55. In what follows we concentrate on what happens when you have simply put "unfair dismissal".
Item 2. Your name and address, telephone number and date of birth.
Item 3. If you have a representative her name can go down here. Note that all letters will then be sent to the named representative only, and *not to you.*

You can put down your *helper's* name here — this doesn't bind her to being your representative — it

48

depends on who you want to deal with the case before the hearing. (If you do this you will have to inform the tribunal at the hearing that you are *not* being represented).

Item 4.. Name of respondent. This is the name and address of your boss. Make sure that you give the name and registered address of the firm that actually employs and pays you. Eg. "Sam Brown & Co. (Brewers) Ltd.", not "the manager, Prince Charles pub". Crown

Item 5. This is where you actually worked, eg "Prince Charles pub, Crown Street, Leeds 11".

Item 6. The title of your job, eg "bar person".

Item 7. Dates when you started and finished the job. If there is any doubt about you having worked long enough to apply, then these dates are very important. Make sure they are correct. If you are uncertain, give approximate dates.

Item 8. Basic wages. Weekly gross wage (ie before tax and National Insurance) *without* overtime, bonuses, etc.

Item 9. Other pay. Put down here average overtime, bonus, etc. Make sure you include all other pay, as it could make a difference to the compensation you get. It is important to mention any pension, superannuation or perks you get.

Item 10. Normal basic hours. This is without overtime.

Item 11. For sex and race discrimination cases only. Put down the date the discrimination happened, or when you first noticed it.

Item 12. Grounds of application. There is a large space on the form for this. For unfair dismissal cases it is usually best to be brief. This isn't the place to give all the details of what happened. Stick to the facts you are absolutely sure about. Remember the facts around the incident dismissed may be only part of important events leading up to the dismissal. In some cases, where there are a lot of clear facts, it can be an advantage to write more and get them all down on the IT1. Just make sure the facts are correct.

In cases where it is up to *the worker* to prove her case, eg constructive dismissal, unfair selection for redundancy, dismissal for trade union membership or activities, unfairly dismissed after a strike, then you need to give slightly more detail.

Item 13. For dismissal cases only. *Leave it blank.* Where you feel it relevant to say what the real reasons were, you can do this in item 12 anyway.

Item 14. Refers to unfair dismissal cases only. If you win, you can either get your job back (called "reinstatement" or "re-engagement") or get money as compensation. The difference between reinstatement and re-engagement is:

Reinstatement re-engagement and compensation

reinstatement means you go back to your old job as if you'd never been sacked (you keep "continuity of employment"). You will get paid for the period in between, plus any rises, and your employment rights carry on with no break in your service (s.69(2) and(3) EPCA. Also see s.70(2)). This is what is meant when the *tribunal* order reinstatement. If reinstatement is arrived at through a settlement, you may have to argue about the terms and include them in the written agreement.

re-engagement means you go back to work for your old boss or an associated firm, but not necessarily in the same job or on the same terms. The new job should be *"comparable and suitable",* and the terms should be *as favourable as before.* You will get paid for the interval in-between plus other money benefits, unless the tribunal decides you were partly to blame, when these are likely to be reduced. Your employment rights continue with no break. (s.69(4) and (6) EPCA and reg. 4, Labour Relations (Continuity of Employment) Regulations 1976).

So if you want your job back, fill in "reinstatement". Leave it up to the IT to decide that re-engagement is more 'just'. If you don't want to go back, or if you have got another job, fill in "compensation". Or if you want to leave your options open, put "I am prepared to consider any of the 3 remedies".

DON'T FORGET TO SIGN AND DATE YOUR APPLICATION. KEEP A PHOTOCOPY.

Where To Send IT   **Send off your application to the Central Office of the Industrial Tribunals** (COIT) in London, Glasgow or

ORIGINATING APPLICATION TO AN INDUSTRIAL TRIBUNAL

IMPORTANT: DO NOT FILL IN THIS FORM UNTIL YOU
HAVE READ THE NOTES FOR GUIDANCE.
THEN COMPLETE ITEMS I, 2,4 AND 12
AND ALL OTHER ITEMS RELEVANT TO YOUR CASE,
AND SEND THE FORM TO THE FOLLOWING ADDRESS

For Official Use Only	
Case Number	

To: THE SECRETARY OF THE TRIBUNALS
CENTRAL OFFICE OF THE INDUSTRIAL TRIBUNALS (ENGLAND AND WALES)
93 EBURY BRIDGE ROAD, LONDON SWIW 8RE   Telephone: 01 730 9161

I   I hereby apply for a decision of a Tribunal on the following question. **(STATE HERE THE QUESTION TO BE DECIDED BY A TRIBUNAL. EXPLAIN THE GROUNDS OVERLEAF).**

    Whether I was unfairly dismissed.

2   My name is (Mr/~~Mrs/Miss~~ Surname in block capitals first):—

    SHAW Harold

    My address is:—   4 Water Lane, Bristol 6

    Telephone No. ————

    My date of birth is   6.4.44

3   If a representative has agreed to act for you in this case please give his or her name and address below and note that further communications will be sent to your representative and not to you   (See Note 4)

    Name of Representative:—

    Address:—

    Telephone No.

4   **(a)** Name of respondent(s) (in block capitals) ie the employer, person or body against whom a decision is sought *(See Note 3)*

    Drainaway Ltd.,

    Address(es)   Bath Street Works, Bath Street, Bath.

    Telephone No.   0225 446400/4

    (b) Respondent's relationship to you for the purpose of the application (eg employer, trade union, employment agency, employer recognising the union making application, etc).   Employer

5   Place of employment to which this application relates, or place where act complained about took place.

    at above address

6   My occupation or position held / applied for, or other relationship to the respondent named above (eg user of a service supplied in relation to employment).

    Van driver

7   Dates employment began about January 1977   and *(if appropriate)* ended   20.5.80

8   **(a)** Basic wages / salary   £61

    (b) Average take home pay   £62

9   Other remuneration or benefits   overtime £16 average

10   Normal basic weekly hours of work   40

11   (In an application under the Sex Discrimination Act or the Race Relations Act) Date on which action complained of took place or first came to my knowledge

12   You are required to set out the grounds for your application below, giving full particulars of them.

> I was unfairly dismissed. I was sacked on the spot by the Works
> Manager over a remark I had made to an employee of a firm I
> collected waste cardboard from. At the same time I was handed a
> letter of warning from my boss; this was the first I had ever
> received. I think I was a good worker for this company.

13   If you wish to state what in your opinion was the reason for your dismissal, please do so here.

14   If the Tribunal decides that you were unfairly dismissed, please state which of the following you would
prefer: reinstatement, re-engagement or compensation. (Before answering this question please consult
the leaflet "Dismissal — Employees Rights", or, "Unfairly Dismissed?".

     Compensation

Signature _Kenneth Shaw_   Date 20.6.80

Belfast, depending on which country you live in (address in Appendix A). **Remember, to be within the time limit, it must be RECEIVED by COIT by that deadline date. Alternatively, if it is very close to the deadline, you can try taking it directly to your Regional Office of Industrial Tribunals (ROIT)** (addresses in Appendix A). Beware — some ROITs have been known to refuse it. **It will be accepted if it is stamped as "received" by the last possible day.**

Wait for written reasons

If you have written to your boss asking him for written reasons for dismissal (see page 55), **then wait 14 days, plus a few days to allow for postage, before sending off your IT1, unless you are close to the time limit. If you don't receive them, then add "unreasonable refusal to supply written reasons for dismissal" to Item 1 of the IT1.**

What Happens Next

COIT is basically a clearing house for applications. It receives your application and checks it to make sure you are eligible to apply to an IT and that you've filled in the IT1 correctly. **If everything's OK, your application is registered and given a case number.** If there is some doubt, you will be asked for more details. If an application is clearly for something an IT has no power to give, eg someone applying about unfair dismissal who has not worked long enought to apply, then you will be sent a letter of explanation. You will be asked if you still wish your application to be registered — the answer would generally be "No". An out-of-time application will usually proceed in the normal way, but a *"preliminary hearing"* will be held to decide whether your application can be heard or not — see page 112.

COIT then sends your application to ROIT. ROIT now takes over and deals entirely with your application. ROIT starts off two procedures:
1. It sends a copy of your IT1 to your boss, and this begins the process towards a tribunal hearing.
2. It sends a copy of your IT1 to ACAS, and this begins the process towards a possible settlement and avoiding an IT hearing.

Time scale

Amending your application

Providing More Information

The approximate time scale, at the time of writing, after you send off your IT1 (unfair dismissal cases) is:

2/5 weeks – you receive a copy of your boss's reply (the IT3 form).

3/6 weeks – ACAS contacts you.

4/6 weeks – possible preliminary hearing or pre-hearing assessment (see page 112).

– you get proposed dates for the hearing (some regions only).

5/7 weeks – the date is set for the hearing.

8/10 weeks – the IT hearing takes place.

If you want to alter the grounds of your application (eg changing one about redundancy pay to unfair dismissal), you can write to ROIT to ask the IT to consider this. So long as you applied in time and the basic details were included in your original application, the IT will consider your changes. The IT is supposed to consider all the circumstances of the case, in particular any injustice or hardship which might be caused by allowing, or refusing, the changes. (COCKING v SANDHURST (STATIONERS) LTD. (1974)ICR 650; (1975)ITR 6: NIRC).

You can ask for your application to be amended right up to the day of the hearing itself, but the sooner you ask the better your changes of having the change allowed.

New regulations (rules 3(2)(ii) and 4, ITRP Regs) **allow your boss to ask you for further details — called "further particulars" — of your case even before he sends any reply to your claim.** If you do not provide this information, your boss can ask the tribunal to dismiss your application. However, you can instead ask the tribunal for permission to ignore your boss's request, if you feel you have given sufficient detail in your IT1 and he is just trying to delay your application or put you off applying. If the request appears reasonable, or if the tribunal order you to give the details, you must give them. At the time of writing, it is not clear how common these requests for more information will be. Also see page 94. If you receive one, don't let it put you off

54

continuing with your case; if you are in doubt about how much detail to supply, get advice.

Page 94 gives more details on the procedure your boss has to follow to get an order from the tribunal.

Special Note — Section 53 Claim

When a person is sacked, she has the right to be given in writing the reasons for her dismissal, as long as she has worked for 26 weeks (s.53EPCA). So if your boss didn't give you this, write asking him to put in writing the reasons why you were sacked.

Claim to a tribunal

If your boss unreasonably refuses to provide you with written reasons, or if the reasons given are inadequate or untrue, you can apply to an IT. This can form a separate application and you could apply about this even if you cannot apply about unfair dismissal. Or you can include it as a separate claim on your unfair dismissal application, or you can write to amend your unfair dismissal application to include this extra complaint, if it has already been sent in. The time limit for claiming is 3 months from when you were dismissed. Obviously, it is not anywhere near as important as a claim for unfair dismissal, but you could win this claim even if you lost your unfair dismissal case. You get 2 weeks gross wages as compensation if

'INCOMPETENCE?' I'd like to see you get 'em like that!'

55

you win this claim.

As case law currently stands, a failure to reply within the 14 days time limit is not necessarily an "unreasonable refusal".

L did not provide written reasons with 14 days, but eventually (after 21 days) did so. The EAT, allowing an appeal by L, held that whilst a stage may be reached when inaction must be understood as an unreasonable refusal to provide written reasons, there was insufficient evidence in this case to show that there had been such unreasonable refusal; s.53 should be rigidly construed and should only be applied when the evidence clearly indicated an unreasonable refusal.

CHARLES LANG & SONS LTD v AUBREY. (1978)ICR 168; (1977)IRLR 354: EAT.

If you are saying his reasons are untrue or inadequate, then YOU must prove that. "Inadequate" means that he did not give enough specific information. For example, he simply replied you were sacked for misconduct, without giving any details about this. The written statement of reasons for dismissal must contain those reasons, with referring to other documents.

The EAT held that, although the employers were entitled to refer to other documents, the written statement must disclose the reasons for dismissal, and must be of such a kind that the employee or anyone to whom he showed it could know from reading the document itself why the employee had been dismissed.

HORSLEY SMITH & SHERRY LTD v DUTTON. (1977)IRLR 172; (1977)ICR 594: EAT.

Reasons given to you verbally are not enough. By law, they must be in writing.

There are two different purposes in asking for written reasons, and how you go about writing depends on what your purpose is.

If you are considering such a "section 53 claim", then you could write to your employer: "Dear Sir or Madam, Please send me full written reasons why I was dismissed. If I do not hear from you within 14 days I will assume that you are refusing to provide me with these reasons. Yours faithfully, etc." Keep a photocopy or a carbon copy and send it by recorded delivery.

Informal approach   However, **you may prefer a more informal approach, in the hope that your boss will reply less cautiously. Sometimes an employer will give different reasons, and often more direct and straightforward reasons, than a more carefully worded response after you have applied about unfair dismissal on the IT1. Any difference in his reasons can be used to your advantage at the hearing.** Write in your own hand-writing: "Dear Sir or Madam, Please send me in writing the reasons why I was dismissed. Yours faithfully, etc". Keep a carbon or a photocopy. Of course, this informal approach could also eventually lead to a section 53 claim as above, although there would probably be more difficulty in showing unreasonable refusal to reply.

When to write   In either case, send off your letter asking for written reasons immediately, but *hold back* your unfair dismissal application until the 14 days are up (unless you are close to the time limit).

Referral at this stage (for helpers only).   If you have helped an applicant fill in the IT1, but do not have time to help her prepare her case, you could refer her to a solicitor for help with preparation under the Green Form scheme (see page 22).Check her eligibility for this. Remember there is no legal aid for the solicitor to represent the applicant at the hearing. She would have to pay for that. Find out which solicitors are good on employment law in your area.

Find out if there is a Free Representation service or Tribunal Representation Unit in your area (see page 21), willing to represent in the particular case. The solicitor may agree to prepare a 'brief' (see page 119) for the free representative. Or is there a solicitor who would represent for a low fee?

If there is no good service to refer an applicant to, we encourage you to continue with the case yourself. Consider helping with preparation at least, even if you do not feel able to attend the hearing. Your help should be better than none at all (see page 4); you will build up your experience; and you could get advice over the phone from a Tribunal Representation Unit, law centre or Free Representation Unit.

8. OTHER PROBLEMS

You will usually have a few other things to sort out, as well as the IT application:

Notice Of Dismissal

Check that you got the correct notice, or pay instead of notice (called "pay in lieu of notice"). As long as you worked for 4 weeks, the *legal minimum* notice your employer must give you is one week. And after working for 2 years, you get an extra week for each year of working; ie, 2 weeks after 2 years, 5 weeks after 5 years, etc (up to a limit of 12 weeks after 12 years). This is the legal minimum notice (s.49(1) EPCA). It is called "statutory notice". If your contract says you get more notice, then you get more. You may find your boss tries to justify an instant dismissal without notice on the grounds of "gross misconduct" (see page 41). If you are claiming unfair dismissal, you will undoubtedly contest this. You can only be sacked without notice or pay in lieu of notice for *gross* (very serious) misconduct

Holiday Pay

Check that you received the right holiday pay. There is no statutory legal entitlement to holiday pay, unless your job is covered by a Wages Council (see page 183. If it is you can check your entitlement by phoning the Wages Council Inspectorate). Normally holiday pay depends entirely on the holiday agreement in your contract, or the usual holidays given by your firm. If you don't get the right amount, sue your boss in the County Court — see page 182.

Unemployment Benefit

You may have hassles about your unemployment benefit. If you are sacked for misconduct or leave voluntarily, you are likely to be suspended and later disqualified from unemployment benefit for up to 6 weeks. Check any letter you have had from the DE. Does it say you are "SUSPENDED from unemployment benefit pending enquiries", or that you are "DISQUALIFIED from unemployment benefit"? Ring up the DE office and find out if you are not sure.

Suspended

If you are suspended, it means that an Insurance Officer of the DE is looking into the circumstances in which you left your last job and that no decision has actually been made yet. You cannot appeal yet. It can take several weeks for the Insurance Officer to collect information and make a decision. In this period you may be sent a form (called a UB86) asking you questions about how you left your job and asking for your comments on your boss's version of how you left. *Be careful* what you say on this form if you are applying to an IT. Your boss may get a copy of what you say. It is probably bad to give away your case. Give the true story without going into much detail and *keep a photocopy* of both what your employer has said and what you say, as this may be vital evidence if you go to an IT.

Disqualified

When a decision is made, you may be disqualified from unemployment benefit but you can appeal to a National Insurance Local Tribunal about this. There is a 21 day time limit for appealing. Make sure you appeal within this time limit, which runs from the date of the written decision. The IT case is usually more important, and you can ask for this appeal to be heard after the IT hearing to avoid airing the circumstances of your dismissal prematurely. If you lose at the IT, you can still go to the Local Tribunal as one tribunal has nothing to do with the other.

Supplementary Benefit

Don't forget that while you are suspended or disqualified from unemployment benefit you may still be entitled to supplementary benefit (often called "social security"), although your personal allowance may be cut by 20% or 40%. You should claim supplementary benefit as soon as you are unemployed. Ask for form B1 from your local DE office.

If your supplementary benefit is cut you can appeal:
1. to a Supplementary Benefit Appeal Tribunal about the cut (on grounds of hardship *or* that a wrong decision has been made).
2. to a National Insurance Local Tribunal about the disqualification.

Keep a record of the unemployment/supplementary

benefit you get, in case you need to work out compensation when reaching a settlement (see page 61).

You can get information and advice on unemployment and supplementary benefit problems from advice centres, CABs, law centres, trade unions, etc.

9. STARTING THE CASE: CHECKLIST

Have you done the following:
1. Sent off for written reasons?
2. Written a full account of what happened (for your own or your helper's use — not to be sent to the IT)?
3. Sent off your IT1 to COIT within the time limit?
4. Sorted out notice, holiday pay, social security benefits, etc?

Compensation

You have sent off your IT1. The Regional Office of Industrial Tribunals (ROIT) will automatically send a copy of it to your boss and to ACAS. ACAS will offer to try and help get a settlement between the two parties, worker and boss, in all IT cases (except redundancy payment applications). They will contact you about 3/6 weeks after you send off your IT1.

Need To Work Out Compensation

For unfair dismissal cases, you can work out what is the most compensation you could get if you won your case. Try to do this NOW, as you will need an estimate for any negotiation. It is wise to do this even if you want your job back. Your firm might offer compensation and you may want to consider this and bargain with them about how much. If you are doubtful about your calculations, ACAS will often help you work out compensation when they come to see you.

If you win your unfair dismissal case and the tribunal award you compensation and not reinstatement, **the compensation you get is made up of a basic award plus a compensatory award** (s.72 EPCA). The maximum basic award is £3,900 and the maximum compensatory award is £6,250 (present figures) — a possible total of

£10,150. There is also the possibility of a later 'additional award'

The Basic Award

This and redundancy payments are worked out in the same way. The amount you get depends on 3 things: how long you worked, your age, and your basic gross weekly pay.

Time worked

1. *How long you worked.*
Take the date your job finished and count the number of full years you worked for that firm. (Note: the date your job ended might not be the date you were sacked. The right date could include the correct statutory (not contractual) notice, which your boss may or may not have given you. If you are given pay in lieu of notice (eg 6 weeks pay instead of 6 weeks notice), the date your job finishes is still the end of your notice period (the end of the 6 weeks). See "effective date of termination", page ii).

Eg: You were sacked without notice on July 15th 1980. You started on August 1st 1976. So you were due the legal minimum notice for 3 years work, which is 3 weeks. This brings your finishing date forward to August 5th 1980 — so you have worked for 4 full years.

Your age

Weekly pay

2. *Your age.*
For each full year you worked for the firm, you get from ½ to 1½ weeks pay, depending on your age:

* 18–21 years old — ½ weeks pay.
* 22–40 years old — 1 weeks pay.
* 41–64 years old — 1½ weeks pay.
There is a ready-reckoner overleaf.

3. *Weekly pay.*
This is your gross basic wage, ie befor deductions. It includes bonus, but not overtime. (Except if overtime is compulsory, when you include the average amount for the last 12 weeks). The maximum weekly pay allowed is at present £130. What you write down will either be your last week's gross pay, or else the average amount over the last 12 weeks. (The EPA, schedule 4, explains the calculation).

		SERVICE (years) 2	3	4	5	6	7	8	9	10	11	12	13	14	15	16	17	18	19	20
AGE (years)	**20**	1	1	1	1	—														
	21	1	1½	1½	1½	1½	—													
	22	1	1½	2	2	2	2	—												
	23	1½	2	2½	3	3	3	3	—											
	24	2	2½	3	3½	4	4	4	4	—										
	25	2	3	3½	4	4½	5	5	5	5	—									
	26	2	3	4	4½	5	5½	6	6	6	6	—								
	27	2	3	4	5	5½	6	6½	7	7	7	7	—							
	28	2	3	4	5	6	6½	7	7½	8	8	8	8	—						
	29	2	3	4	5	6	7	7½	8	8½	9	9	9	9	—					
	30	2	3	4	5	6	7	8	8½	9	9½	10	10	10	10	—				
	31	2	3	4	5	6	7	8	9	9½	10	10½	11	11	11	11	—			
	32	2	3	4	5	6	7	8	9	10	10½	11	11½	12	12	12	12	—		
	33	2	3	4	5	6	7	8	9	10	11	11½	12	12½	13	13	13	13	—	
	34	2	3	4	5	6	7	8	9	10	11	12	12½	13	13½	14	14	14	14	—
	35	2	3	4	5	6	7	8	9	10	11	12	13	13½	14	14½	15	15	15	15
	36	2	3	4	5	6	7	8	9	10	11	12	13	14	14½	15	15½	16	16	16
	37	2	3	4	5	6	7	8	9	10	11	12	13	14	15	15½	16	16½	17	17
	38	2	3	4	5	6	7	8	9	10	11	12	13	14	15	16	16½	17	17½	18
	39	2	3	4	5	6	7	8	9	10	11	12	13	14	15	16	17	17½	18	18½
	40	2	3	4	5	6	7	8	9	10	11	12	13	14	15	16	17	18	18½	19
	41	2	3	4	5	6	7	8	9	10	11	12	13	14	15	16	17	18	19	19½
	42	2½	3½	4½	5½	6½	7½	8½	9½	10½	11½	12½	13½	14½	15½	16½	17½	18½	19½	20½
	43	3	4	5	6	7	8	9	10	11	12	13	14	15	16	17	18	19	20	21
	44	3	4½	5½	6½	7½	8½	9½	10½	11½	12½	13½	14½	15½	16½	17½	18½	19½	20½	21½
	45	3	4½	6	7	8	9	10	11	12	13	14	15	16	17	18	19	20	21	22
	46	3	4½	6	7½	8½	9½	10½	11½	12½	13½	14½	15½	16½	17½	18½	19½	20½	21½	22½
	47	3	4½	6	7½	9	10	11	12	13	14	15	16	17	18	19	20	21	22	23
	48	3	4½	6	7½	9	10½	11½	12½	13½	14½	15½	16½	17½	18½	19½	20½	21½	22½	23½
	49	3	4½	6	7½	9	10½	12	13	14	15	16	17	18	19	20	21	22	23	24
	50	3	4½	6	7½	9	10½	12	13½	14½	15½	16½	17½	18½	19½	20½	21½	22½	23½	24½
	51	3	4½	6	7½	9	10½	12	13½	15	16	17	18	19	20	21	22	23	24	25
	52	3	4½	6	7½	9	10½	12	13½	15	16½	17½	18½	19½	20½	21½	22½	23½	24½	25½
	53	3	4½	6	7½	9	10½	12	13½	15	16½	18	19	20	21	22	23	24	25	26
	54	3	4½	6	7½	9	10½	12	13½	15	16½	18	19½	20½	21½	22½	23½	24½	25½	26½
	55	3	4½	6	7½	9	10½	12	13½	15	16½	18	19½	21	22	23	24	25	26	27
	56	3	4½	6	7½	9	10½	12	13½	15	16½	18	19½	21	22½	23½	24½	25½	26½	27½
	57	3	4½	6	7½	9	10½	12	13½	15	16½	18	19½	21	22½	24	25	26	27	28
	58	3	4½	6	7½	9	10½	12	13½	15	16½	18	19½	21	22½	24	25½	26½	27½	28½
	59	3	4½	6	7½	9	10½	12	13½	15	16½	18	19½	21	22½	24	25½	27	28	29
Men only	**60**	3	4½	6	7½	9	10½	12	13½	15	16½	18	19½	21	22½	24	25½	27	28½	29½
Men only	**61**	3	4½	6	7½	9	10½	12	13½	15	16½	18	19½	21	22½	24	25½	27	28½	30
Men only	**62**	3	4½	6	7½	9	10½	12	13½	15	16½	18	19½	21	22½	24	25½	27	28½	30
Men only	**63**	3	4½	6	7½	9	10½	12	13½	15	16½	18	19½	21	22½	24	25½	27	28½	30
Men only	**64**	3	4½	6	7½	9	10½	12	13½	15	16½	18	19½	21	22½	24	25½	27	28½	30

Working it out is often straightforward, but it can be complicated, eg. if there are different amounts of overtime each week. You may need to write for your last 12 weeks wage slips, or you could write in a provisional figure to check out further later.

Eg: You are a piece worker. Over the last 12 weeks before notice was given, your TOTAL gross pay (excluding overtime, which is not in your contract) was £1080. This was (without overtime) for a total of 480 hours work. Your average hourly rate is then 1080 divided by 480 which equals £2.25 per hour. Your average weekly hours without overtime are 480 divided by 12 which equals 40 hours. So a week's pay is 40 times £2.25 = £90.

Near to retirement

People in their last year before state retirement age get a bad deal (women aged 59, men aged 64). Their basic award is reduced as follows:

Work out the number of full months between your 59th and 64th birthday and the date your job finished. Take the amount of basic award you have worked out so far. Divide this by 12, then multiply it by the number of months.

Eg: You are a woman and were 59 and 9months exactly when sacked. Your weeks pay in £60. Your award so far is 10 full years @ 1½ weeks = 15 × £60 = £900. A twelfth of this = £75. Multiply by 9 for the nine months over 59 = £675. Then your basic award is £900 − £675 = £225.

Young workers

Employees over 16 and under 18 with at least 52 weeks service get a basic award of ½ a week's pay per year (s.9(3) EA). This does not apply for redundancy payments.

Reduction of the basic award

The basic award you have worked out will be reduced in two circumstances:
1. If you have already received a redundancy payment, this will be offset from the basic award and may cancel it out completely (s.73(9) EPCA).
2. **If an IT decides that the dismissal was partly your fault, then they will reduce the basic award (s.9(4) EA). They can also reduce it if you unreasonably refuse an**

offer of reinstatement (s.8(4) EA). They will reduce it by the percentage they think you are to blame. So if they think you are half to blame, they reduce it by half — 50%. Reductions of over 80% are rare.

Work out the basic award without allowing for this reduction for now. We'll deal with this later — see page 69

C assaulted another employee when provoked. He was interviewed and told to report back for a formal hearing on the following Monday. When he didn't turn up, he was dismissed by letter. Meanwhile, C had written explaining his version of the incident and that he had been ill on the day of the hearing. The dismissal was found to be unfair as R had not given C a hearing after getting his letter, but the tribunal reduced compensation on the grounds of contributory fault.
CHYRSTIE v ROLLS ROYCE. (1976)IRLR 336: EAT.

Compensatory Award

This concerns your personal monetary loss due to unfair dismissal. You must tell the tribunal about *all* the losses you want to be compensated for, otherwise they many not consider them. You can claim compensation for the following losses:

Present loss of earnings

1. *Present loss of earnings* — from when you were sacked to the date (or likely date) of the IT hearing. (This category is called 'present loss' to separate it from 'future loss' — see below). In working out your loss of pay you have to subtract:

* the amount of unemployment and supplementary benefit received up to the hearing date. (If compensation is worked out by the IT you won't need to work this out; it will be "recouped" directly by the DHSS/DE (see below). But if a settlement is reached you will have to work this out yourself).
* any wages in lieu of notice.
* any other "ex-gratia payments" (eg golden handshake).
* any other wages from a job you've gone on to (eg part-time earnings).

Even if you get another job soon after being sacked, you can still claim some loss of earnings if the new job has lower wages. Claim the difference in wages between your old and new jobs.

To work out your loss, take your weekly NET pay (after deductions for tax and National Insurance contributions but including average overtime, bonus, etc). Multiplyit by the relevant number of weeks. (If you were due to get a wage rise soon after you were sacked, or promotion to a new grade, then include this higher pay from the date it would have started).

Recoupment and settlement

If you have been getting unemployment benefit or supplementary benefit while you were unemployed, the amount of benefit you received may have to be paid back to the DHSS/DE by your boss. This is called "recoupment" of benefit. Any benefit "recouped" (or clawed back) is paid by your boss to the DHSS/DE, out of the 'loss of earnings' part (or "prescribed element") of the total compensation he is due to pay you.

If you settle through ACAS or privately (so the tribunal do not make an *order* for compensation), then no social security benefits will be recouped. This means your boss may be willing to settle for a larger amount than otherwise, as he will not have to pay anything to the DHSS/DE. For example, if the tribunal award you £800 compensation, your boss might end up paying the DHSS £200 recoupment and you £600. If you settle between yourselves for £700, then (as there is no recoupment) both of you end up £100 better off.

Future loss of earnings

2. *Future loss of earnings.* If you are still unemployed at the date of the hearing, you should claim loss of earnings for the time it should take to get another job. Or if you have got another job, but it is less well paid, claim for the difference in wages for a certain time after the hearing. In practice, the future loss period varies enormously – from a couple of weeks to over 3 months. You should get longer if there is less demand for your particular skill.

To work out the amount of future loss you think you should be entitled to, again take your weekly net pay (including any wage rise or promotion you would have got in the future) and multiply by the number of weeks you estimate.

Do not subtract future social security benefits because you will not be entitled to unemployment, sickness, invalidity or supplementary benefit for any period of future loss awarded. This period is not treated as days of unemployment (Social Security (Unemployment, Sickness and Invalidity Benefit) Regulations 1975 (as amended) reg. 7(1)(1)(iii)). If, however, you can agree on the future loss between you through a settlement you may both end up better off — see page 66.

Loss of job prospects

Your job prospects may be worse after being sacked. Eg: if you were sacked for being an active trade unionist, you may now be blacklisted by other firms in the area. It is up to you to argue for what you think you should get, but note there is no compensation for injured feelings. This can be quite difficult to get.

Loss of other benefits

3. *Loss of Benefits.* Your dismissal may mean the loss of other perks that went with the job, eg. free house, car or luncheon vouchers. Include the value of these in your compensation.

Pension rights

4. *Loss of pension rights.*

The Government Actuary's Department has produced guidelines for working out pension loss. Copies can be obtained free from COIT, if you give your IT case number. However, they are very detailed and tribunals will prefer a simpler approach.

There are two types of pension loss:

a) Loss of pension already earned. This is made up of contributions paid by your employer and usually also by you. (If your pension is a deferred pension, then there will be no loss here — all the contributions will be frozen until you retire. This affects everyone over 26 who has contributed for at least 5 years since April 1975).

Take the total sum of contributions paid. Usually your employer will have paid back your contributions — this should include interest. If so, only add up his contributions. The contributions you have not received are called the 'capital sum'. Next take the rate of interest. Working out the exact amount is very complicated. To get the rough amount, divide the capital sum by the rate of interest. Add this amount to the capital sum. This rough way makes the total a bit high, so knock off a small amount. This is the total earned pension loss.

If you are near to retirement there is a simpler way. Take the total lump sum your pension would have been when you retired. Subtract the contributions still due. This gives the total loss of earned pension.

It may be possible to transfer the pension to a new job. This is unusual, but if so there is no loss.

b) Loss of future pension. This cannot usually be simply worked out. If there is not pension scheme at your new job, then you lose out by not getting the employer's contribution, and also by not being able to pay your own contributions tax free. If there is a pension scheme, it will probably be different. Your loss will be the difference between your future benefits in the old scheme, had you not been sacked, and your future benefits in the new scheme, taking into account the relative amounts you and your employer pay in each situation. You can look at the Government Actuary's guidelines on this, or just have the facts ready for the tribunal to work it out at the hearing.

Loss of other rights 5. *Loss of other rights*. You have to work 12 months to be protected against unfair dismissal and 2 years to get a redundancy payment. These rights will be lost by being sacked, and you have to start again with your new job. ITs often only award £10-£30 for this loss. At the hearing, you can argue that this is not enough, particularly with inflation and the recent increase in the period before you again have the right to claim unfair dismissal. You could also ake for a payment for loss of maternity rights, pregnant or not (if relevant), but this is not commonly given.

If you worked for one firm for a while, you were entitled to a long period of notice of dismissal, eg 5 weeks if you worked for 5 years. In a new job you will only be entitled to one week's notice. ITs sometimes value this loss at about half the money you would lose.

So after 5 years you would lose 4 weeks notice, so the IT awards 2 weeks pay. But if you don't draw the IT's attention to this loss, you may not get anything.

Expenses of looking for work

6. *Expenses of looking for work.* Trying to get another job can be expensive, eg fares, phone calls, stamps. Keep a note of these as they mount up.

ADD UP THE TOTAL UNDER THESE DIFFERENT HEADINGS.

Reduction of the compensatory award

Like the basic award, your compensatory award may be reduced in two circumstances:

a) *Contributory factor.* If an IT thinks the dismissal was unfair but partly your own fault, then they will reduce the compensatory award (as well as the basic award) by a percentage — see page   . This is the most difficult factor to estimate.

'I don't care what you drink lass — if you hurt yourself you'll not get a penny from this firm'

(ACKNOWLEGEMENT to GUINNESS Co.)

b) *Mitigation of loss.* An IT can also reduce your compensatory award if they think you have not tried hard enough to get another job, or have unreasonably refused an offer of reinstatement or re-engagement. You should be signing on as unemployed and actively looking for work while waiting for your case to come up. (It is usually reasonable to not accept a job offered, at least in the first place, if it involves less pay or status, as you are entitled to protect your skill and status. If your job was abnormally highly paid, however, you would probably be expected to take a lower paid job and rely on a claim for prolonged partial loss earnings).

Total Compensation

ADD YOUR ESTIMATES OF THE BASIC AND COMPENSATORY AWARDS TOGETHER. This is the total compensation you reckon you are entitled to without taking account of possible reduction by a tribunal for contributory fault.

The big problem with working out compensation is that some things are concrete while others are not — eg how do you know how much contributory fault to allow for? The thing is to get some idea of compensation rather than an amount down to the last sixpence. Employers' and your ideas of contributory fault may be worlds apart. It is a good idea to work out two figures:

1. Compensation without any contributory fault.
2. Some guess at an amount you are willing to come down to in any settlement. How much are you prepared to say you were to blame — 90%; 30%; 10% ?

If you have made a separate section 53 claim (see page 55), then add to your final calculation·2 weeks gross pay.

Keep your notes of how you worked out the compensation for any negotiation; for when you see ACAS, and for the IT hearing. Be ready to give good reasons why you think you are entitled to the amount you want under each heading.

See the example of working out compensation on page 71.

Example of working out compensation.

Basic award

4 full years employed; age 42; gross weekly wage £90

So basic award = $4 \times 1\frac{1}{2} \times £90$

$= £540$

Compensatory award

still unemployed.

1. Present loss of earnings: 9 weeks between sacking and hearing date; net pay £72 a week.

   So loss of earnings = $9 \times £72 = £648$

   But £315 benefit will have been received

   So present loss = $£648 - £315 = £333$

2. Future loss of earnings:

   conversation with Job Centre suggests a possible further 8 weeks unemployed. (get letter to confirm)

   So future loss = $8 \times £72 = £576$

3. Other benefits — none

4. Pension rights — no pension

5. Loss of other rights: try for £50 unfair dismissal loss, etc. plus 1½ weeks pay for loss of notice rights = £108

   So loss of other rights = £158

6. Expenses of looking for work = about £15

   So compensatory award = $£333 + £576 + £158 + £15$

   $= £1082$

Total compensation

$= £540 + £1082$

$= £1600$ approx

[If private settlement (no recoupment) try for £1750]

If I allow 20% contributory fault, total compensation will be $£1600 - £300$ approx.

$= £1300$

71

1. INTRODUCTION

This section is called "Negotiation and Settlement". The next section is called "Preparation for the Hearing". **In "Negotiation and Settlement" we deal with an unfair dismissal case which is settled and never gets to an IT hearing. In "Preparation for the Hearing" we go through an unfair dismissal case which is not settled and goes on to an IT hearing. Remember, with a real case these two procedures will be happening AT THE SAME TIME.**

Negotiation is very common in IT cases. About 3 times more unfair dismissal cases are settled through negotiation than end up at a tribunal hearing. The present recoupment regulations (see page 66) and the cost of hiring solicitors are both important factors in encouraging negotiation to save money all round.

Negotiation may have arisen earlier (see page 17). **This section focuses on the occasion when negotiation more normally arises; after the IT1 has been sent in. There are two possibilities for negotiation here:**
1. through ACAS.
2. directly with your boss or his representative,

through your helper or representative. The more experienced a helper or representative is, the more likely this sort of negotiation is and the more fruitful it is likely to be.

In what follows, we cover negotiation through ACAS. However, many of the pointers given here will also be useful if you are negotiating directly. In any negotiation you are first going to need a clear idea of what remedy you want. If compensation is possible, then you need an idea of the amount (see the previous "Compensation" section).

2. NEGOTIATION THROUGH ACAS

Introduction

If you are claiming unfair dismissal, a photocopy of your IT1 and your boss's reply on the IT3 form will be automatically sent to ACAS by ROIT. This is the only information ACAS will receive. it will go to a "conciliation officer" who will try and get a settlement between you and your boss so that a hearing will not be necessary (s.134 EPCA).

What Does ACAS Do?

ACAS stands for the Advisory, Conciliation and Arbitration Service. It is independent of the government, though it gets its money from the government. It was set up by parliament under the Employment Protection Act 1975. ACAS is formally controlled by a Council of a Chairperson and 9 members; 3 from the TUC, 3 from the CBI, and 3 others. ACAS has a head office in London and 8 regional offices (see Appendix A for the one in your area). You hear a lot about ACAS on the news to do with strikes, etc. We are only concerned here with the "conciliation" part of their work for *individual* cases.

ACAS also has an enquiry desk giving advice by phone and to personal callers. And ACAS issues written codes of practice under certain Acts (see Appendix B), which the tribunal has to take into account (see page 101). Eg code of practice 1: "Disciplinary practice and procedure in employment", issued under the EPCA, lays down the disciplinary actions of verbal and written warnings, etc.

73

Role Of ACAS In IT Cases

ACAS try and settle all the different sorts of IT cases, apart from redundancy payments. (The DE has special sections dealing with redundancy payments and insolvency payments). **But 95% of their work is on unfair dismissal cases. They should offer to see both you and the employer separately. You do not have to see them if you are not interested in a settlement, and this will not harm your case when it comes to the hearing.** There is nothing said or written between ACAS and the IT about the negotiations or about any attempt at settlement.

'Are you sure this is the way ACAS usually settles disputes of this kind?'

The IT just assumes agreement was not possible. Also any details which come out during negotiation cannot be stated at the tribunal hearing by either side unless by agreement. And ACAS will not give evidence to the tribunal about negotiations unless it is requested and both sides agree. (The ACAS officer can be a witness at the hearing only about something *you* said to her. You cannot ask her about things your boss said to her).

The ACAS officer is a go-between for the two sides, you and your boss. She has no power to say who is right or wrong, or whether the dismissal was fair or not. That is up to the tribunal to decide. Nor can ACAS impose a settlement. ACAS can, however, point out the weaknesses and strengths of your case. Remember that any offer of settlement she brings is coming from your boss, not from ACAS. The officer is only the messenger.

If there is no chance of agreement and settlement between you and your boss, then the ACAS officer will withdraw. Your case will then go on to an IT hearing. If you change your mind later and would consider a settlement, don't hesitate to contact the ACAS officer again. ACAS will get in touch with your boss with any offer.

Is Negotiation Worth It?

You may think there's no chance of any agreement between you and your boss. Especially if his reply on the IT3 is quite heavy and he obviously intends to fight your claim. You do not have to see or speak to ACAS and it shouldn't harm your case if you don't. (Note that this is different from not following the grievance procedure, which probably would harm your case if you didn't try it – see page 8).

But our advice is that it is useful to see ACAS, even if you think the chances of settlement are remote. But only if you have FIRST thought out your case a bit and calculated compensation. All the details your boss has put on the IT3 may be trivialities if he knows he has a poor case. You may find out extra information about your boss's case. The officer may point out weaknesses in your case. It is useful to know of these weaknesses as you can then work on them to try and remedy them. This can work both ways, however. Some advisers feel that ACAS officers tend to be employer-minded and disclosure of your case tends to be one way: not yours.

What Is Settlement?

Settlement can be compensation or reinstatement. Compensation is much more common. Many unfair dismissal applications (about ⅓) are resolved by the two parties agreeing to settle for a sum of money and therefore not going to the tribunal. Reinstatement is more likely to happen through ACAS than by order of the tribunal (see page   ), probably because it is easier very soon after you have been sacked.

Most settlement agreements state they are in "full and final settlement of this application and of *all other claims* which the applicant could have brought arising out of her contract of employment and termination".

Be careful. If you have any other claim against your boss do not agree to this. For example, if you are suing him for debt in the County Court because he did not give you the holiday pay due to you, or if you are claiming compensation against him for an accident at work. Either make sure that all the money owed to you is included in the settlement, or make sure that the agreement only states "in full and final settlement of this application". Otherwise do not sign it. See the example on page 83).

When is settlement a good idea?

It is a good idea to settle if you can get what you want without going to the IT. If you are seeking compensation this is possible. If you want reinstatement, this is possible but rare. If you also want a good reference to help you get another job, you can try to make this part of the settlement. Insist on having the wording of the reference written into any agreement. (Employers are often quite easily persuaded into giving good references as it doesn't cost them anything). See the example on page 83.

When is settlement a bad idea?

It is a bad idea to settle if you want it publicly recorded that you were sacked unfairly. Many people apply to ITs *on principle* as much as for money or to get their jobs back. They want their names cleared, eg if they've been sacked for theft at work. Most agreements state that the employer "denies liability". In other words, he does not admit that he was at fault and that you were unfairly dismissed. However, if you want your name cleared only so that you can get another job more easily, then try for a good reference as part of the settlement (see above).

Meeting ACAS

Initial contact

The ACAS officer should get in touch with you about 3/6 weeks after the IT1 was sent off. If there is a representative named on the IT1, then ACAS will contact the representative. Otherwise the officer will contact you. Normally she will ring up, if you are on the phone. She will probably want to talk a bit about the case. Don't say much. Arrange a proper meeting where all are present: you, your helper/representative, and ACAS. A full conversation can be had then.

*(For
representatives)*
If you are a representative, you may want to take the initiative in calling ACAS in, especially if dismissal has just occured and some reconsideration is possible before the dust settles. Otherwise, if you are named on the IT1, ACAS should contact you. But beware; sometimes they contact the applicant directly. So tell the applicant not to see or speak to ACAS on her own. If ACAS contacts her, she should refer the officer to you, her representative, and inform you.

(for helpers)
If you are a helper, you may want to take the initiative in calling ACAS in, as described above. If you are not named on the IT1, then ACAS will contact the applicant. Warn her not to meet or speak to ACAS on her own, but to get in touch with you and arrange a meeting with you there too.

Always be present when ACAS talks to the applicant. She may say things which the employer should not know.

(for applicants)
If you are the person applying, ACAS will contact you unless someone is named as your representative on the IT1. If an adviser or trade unionist is helping you with your case, then arrange a meeting with the ACAS officer when they can be there. *Never see ACAS on your own.* You need to be careful what you say, and two people are better than one. Even if your friend only listens and shuts you up if necessary.

If you have a representative named on the IT1, ACAS shouldn't — but sometimes does — get in touch with you instead. Don't talk to them. Tell them to ring your representative not you, and you will see them with your representative present.

What you can say
Anything you say to the ACAS officer could be told to your boss. So be careful what you say. This doesn't mean you should say nothing. You may decide yours is the sort of case where you are quite happy to give a lot of detail. Normally it's best just to give the brief facts of what happened, without going into detail. Only say things you don't mind being told to your boss. If you do want to tell the ACAS officer something which your boss should not know, then state that the information is

"in confidence". The officer should not divulge what you say. Eg; there is a strong point in your favour you don't want your boss to know before the hearing – but you tell the ACAS officer "in confidence". So she knows you have a good case which may persuade your boss to settle. Obviously this system depends on how much you feel you can trust the officer.

Preparation For The Meeting

One good idea is to *jot down the brief facts of what happened,* so that you know exactly what you are going to tell the officer. Otherwise you may ramble on at the meeting and give too much detail.

Include any strong points of your case in the information you give. They should be points which cannot be out-manoevred by your boss. So there's no harm if he gets to know these facts now. Eg; your boss says part of the reason you were sacked was that you were suspected of stealing a stapler from the office. But you have proof that you were not at work that day. Telling ACAS and your boss such strong points will increase the chances of a good settlement.

Work out beforehand whether you or your helper/representative is going to do most of the talking.

Make sure you have worked out the *compensation* – see page 61.

The Meeting Itself

In most regions, the ACAS officer will see your boss first. So when she comes to see you, she will have heard your boss's side of what happened.

The meeting could go as follows:

1. You tell the ACAS officer what happened. Here your written notes are useful. She will ask you further questions about the dismissal. Eg; if you were sacked for lateness, she will ask how often you were late, how late, if there were any warnings, etc.

2. She tells you what your boss has said to her. *Take notes.* Note the differences between what your boss is saying and your side. Note what reasons he is giving for sacking you. *Ask questions* to get more information. You want to come out of this meeting knowing more about what your boss is going to say at the IT hearing.

3. She asks for your replies to what your boss has said,

especially about the reasons your boss has given for sacking you. *Be very careful here. You don't need to answer.* A helper or representative should listen very carefully to your answers, and tell you to shut up if necessary.

4. She goes through the code of practice with you. She will ask about the disciplinary procedure at your workplace, and if you were given any verbal or written warnings. Remember to have worked out the *dates* of any verbal warnings.

5. She asks if you will consider a settlement. If your answer is yes (see page 76), ask if your boss has made any offer. Go through how you worked out the compensation. Ask her if she thinks it correct or not. State to her the terms of settlement you require, eg compensation plus reference, reinstatement, etc.

6. Ask her what she thinks about your case. She is more likely to say the weaknesses. She is less likely to point out the strengths. It's very unlikely she will say to you that your boss has a weak case.

REMEMBER YOU DON'T HAVE TO ANSWER HER QUESTIONS. YOU ARE THERE BY CHOICE. DON'T ANSWER WHAT YOU DON'T WANT TO. ACAS are used to short or evasive answers and should not press you. Perhaps the information required should be kept back until the tribunal hearing.

Offers Of Settlement

After meeting you the ACAS officer will get in touch with your boss again and give him your side of things and tell him what you want in settlement. A few days later you will receive a phone call or letter from the officer stating your boss's response to your offer of settlement. The possible replies are:

No agreement

a) There is no chance of agreement between you and your boss. Either he is not interested in settlement and wants to go to the IT to defend the case, or he is not prepared to consider your terms of settlement. If this happens the ACAS officer will tell you that she cannot help you and she will withdraw.

Nuisance value offer

b) An offer of compensation of £150 or less. This will be just "nuisance value" money. In other words, your boss will pay you that amount to be rid of you. Probably it would cost him more in loss of production or solicitor's fees to go to the hearing, even if he won. Disregard a nuisance value offer, unless:

O.K. Johnson, you win, we'll PAY you the £500 NUISANCE MONEY.

* you have a very weak case, and your helper/representative advises that you have very little chance of winning at the IT.
* the compensation that you would get if you won is less or not much more than the offer, for example if you got another job straight away, or if you were a lot to blame for the sacking.

Possible agreement   c) An offer of compensation of more than £150. This could be a hopeful sign that your boss realises some of the weaknesses in his case. Perhaps the ACAS officer has pointed these out to him; eg that he should have given you a formal warning before sacking you. It may be possible to get a good settlement. It is still likely there will be a large gap between what your boss is offering as compensation and what you think you should get. Don't worry. Stick to your guns. Be prepared to come down a bit, but don't accept an offer that is too low. Use you judgement. If you and your helper/representative think you would get more at the IT, then don't accept unless you cannot face an IT hearing.

Bargaining

If you don't have a helper or representative, use ACAS to carry the offers between you and your boss. It's likely he will have a solicitor to represent him, and ACAS will be dealing with the solicitor. But your helper /representative may prefer to contact your boss or his representative direct (contact the representative if there is one). Explain in detail how you worked out the compensation. Show you know what you are talking about. If you're dealing with a solicitor, don't be put off or pressurised. Solicitors are more used to this sort of bargaining than you. Don't worry. Be clear as to what you want. Tell the solicitor firmly. Or you can always ask ACAS to act as the go-between again.

Miss Jennings has sent a letter saying that since you've replaced her with a silicon chip perhaps you'd prefer to argue the case with one.

Consider getting to the employer before he gets a solicitor on the scene — remember he has his solicitor's fees to consider at the end of it all.

If your boss or his representative will not agree or come close to what you want, then don't accept. Leave it up to the IT.

81

When bargaining, remember to include everything you want in the settlement. A good reference can be more important than the money.

Making The Agreement

If you and your boss agree on a settlement, then ring up the ACAS officer immediately. Get in touch with her even if the bargaining has been direct between your helper/representative and your boss/boss's representative and ACAS have not been involved. ACAS will send out an agreement form (COT 3) for you to sign. There is an example on page 83. The ACAS officer will have written out the terms of the agreement on the form based on what you and your boss have told her.

Agreement form

The agreement form will be sent to your representative if you have one. It should be signed by you or your representative on your behalf. **BEFORE SIGNING THE AGREEMENT, CHECK WHAT IT SAYS.**

Make sure:

* **It includes a time limit for the money to be paid,** either 14 days or at most 28 days.

* **If a good reference is part of it, have the reference in your hands and make sure it is acceptable before you sign.**

* **The agreement is likely to say that the respondent (your boss) is paying you an "ex-gratia" payment without admission of liability in full and final settlement of the IT application. Is this acceptable? See page 75. If you have any other claim against your boss, make sure the agreement is only in settlement of the IT application.**

If the agreement is not right for you in any of these ways, do not sign it. Send it back to ACAS with a letter saying exactly how you want it changed. Only sign the agreement when it is OK for you. You cannot re-open the case if you regret settling later on.

When the agreement is signed by both you and your boss, ACAS send it to ROIT. It goes to an IT Chairperson who formally records the settlement. You will receive a copy of the agreement from ACAS, and a copy of the IT's "decision" signed by the Chairperson from ROIT. The IT "decision" will normally state that the proceedings are adjourned until further order — see page 85

* Equal Pay Act 1970
* Sex Discrimination Act 1975.
* Race Relations Act 1976
* Employment Protection (Consolidation) Act 1978

* AGREEMENT IN RESPECT OF AN APPLICATION MADE TO THE INDUSTRIAL TRIBUNALS

* AGREEMENT IN RESPECT OF A REQUEST FOR CONCILIATION MADE TO THE ADVISORY CONCILIATION
& ARBITRATION SERVICE (NO APPLICATION MADE TO TRIBUNAL AT TIME OF AGREEMENT)

Applicant	Respondent
Name ...Mrs. K.M. Peers...	Name ....Glew Knitwear...
Address ...83 Roxton View...	Address ...101/103 Tead Street,...
...Leeds7...	...Leeds 10...

Settlement reached as a result of conciliation action.

We the undersigned have agreed:

The respondent denies liability and shall pay to the applicant the sum of £372 by 1st November 1980 as an ex-gratia payment in full and final settlement of these proceedings. This settlement takes into account the sum of £28 being the amount due to the respondent from the applicant for goods received on credit. The respondent shall also supply a reference on their headed notepaper in the following agreed terms:

"TO WHOM IT MAY CONCERN:
Mrs K. M. Peers commenced employment on 3rd May 1978 as a book-keeper. She assumed control of the day-to-day running of our accounts, and was promoted to partial management status on March 1st 1978 and rewarded with the use of a company car. Her work was consistently good and her conduct always entirely satisfactory. She left on 12th September 1980 after a period of illness."

Applicant ...Kate Peers... date ...11.10.70...

Respondent ...C. Franshaw... date ...16.10.80...

* Delete inappropriate item

COT 3

What If Your Boss Does Not Follow The Agreement?

What happens if your employer does not pay the sum of money within the stated time? This happens very rarely. But if it does, you must go back to the IT for a hearing of the case.

What to do first

Ring up the ACAS officer and ask her to give your boss a *reminder*, or ring him direct yourself. Say you'll give him 7 days to pay up or else you will go back to the tribunal. After 7 days if no money has come, ring up again and say you're going back to the tribunal unless payment comes by tomorrow morning. If no cheque arrives, take this action.

What happens if you go back to the IT

If you take your case back to an IT, it will be heard from the beginning, just as if settlement had never been made. The IT will hear the case, make a decision, and, if it's in your favour, award reinstatement or compensation. To do this, just write to ROIT saying what has happened, and ask them to fix a date for a tribunal hearing.

Final Word

1. **Don't settle for a lot less than you reckon you're entitled to.**
2. **Try hard to get a good settlement. Going to an IT is not fun, and a settlement may save you a lot of work and worry.**

THE INDUSTRIAL TRIBUNALS

BETWEEN

Applicant/Appellant

Ms B Hinton

AND

Respondent

Super Upholstery Ltd.

DECISION OF THE INDUSTRIAL TRIBUNAL

HELD AT   Leeds   ON   5 July 1980

CHAIRMAN: Mr D N Smith   MEMBERS: Mrs J N Brown
Mr R Jones

DECISION

The unanimous/majority decision of the Tribunal is that all further proceedings on the claim be adjourned generally until further order upon the terms of the agreement as set out in the reasons for the decision.

REASONS

1.   The application was for a finding that the applicant had been unfairly dismissed from her employment with Super Upholstery Ltd.

2.   The tribunal has been informed that the applicant has agreed to accept the sum of £170 together with accrued holiday pay of £78 and one week's pay in lieu of notice offered to her by the respondents in full and final settlement of the applicant's claim and the tribunal was asked therefore to order that all further proceedings on the claim be adjourned generally until further order, payment to be made within 28 days.

_____
Chairman

Decision sent to the parties on
11 July 1980
and entered in the register
C. R. Gillon (Mrs)
for Secretary of the Tribunals.

Preparation of the Case

1. INTRODUCTION

What this section covers

You've sent off your IT1 and received an acknowledgement. It will probably be at least 2 months before the hearing. But there is usually a lot to do before then. There are two sorts of action going on: trying to get a good settlement, dealt with in the last section; and preparing your case for the hearing. These will be happening at the same time. The things we deal with here are:

* Employer's replies, the IT3 in particular.
* Further particulars.
* Documentary evidence.
* Witnesses.
* Dates of the hearing.
* Checking law and case law.
* Checking other problems.
* Preliminary hearing and pre-hearing assessment.

How Much Preparation?

In this handbook we aim to help you to deal with an IT case very fully. This can take a lot of time and you may not want to do it all. That's OK. Do as much as you can. Preparation means you will know the case against you better before the hearing, and there will be very few questions you won't already know the answers to. In general, the more work you do on your case, the more likely you are to win. When you get to the hearing you will be more informed and better prepared. But whether you win or lose is more to do with the strengths and weaknesses of your actual case in relation to the law. Although this work certainly helps, don't worry if you cannot do it all.

If You Are A Helper /Representative

Similarly, it is up to you how much help you give. Even if you are not going to represent the applicant at the hearing, you can help her a lot to prepare her case. How much work you do is up to you, but it does increase the applicant's chances of success. So do as much as you can.

Reminder

Remember, if a person is named as representative on the IT1, all letters and phone calls come to her and not to the applicant. So *keep each other informed* about the progress of the case.

2. INFORMATION FROM YOUR BOSS

Information Apart From the IT3

What information have you got about your boss's case? Before we go on to look at the IT3, is there anything else?

Reasons for dismissal

If you wrote to your boss asking for the reasons in writing why you were sacked (see page 55), **did you get a reply? Or did you receive a letter on dismissal? Or, if you have been suspended or disqualified from unemployment benefit, do you have forms from the DE** (UB86 and others) **on which your boss gives details about the reasons for your leaving work** (see page 59)?

Compare these with the reasons your boss gives for sacking you in the IT3 — see where they point you in terms of getting information and preparing your case. These letters could well be less cautious than anything in the IT3.

The IT3 Form

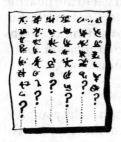

When ROIT receives your IT1 from COIT, they send a copy of it to your boss, plus a letter about it (IT2 form), and an IT3 form on which he puts his reply. **The IT3 is called the "Notice of Appearance". Your boss is meant to return it within 14 days to ROIT, but see below. A copy of it will then be sent to you.** There is an example on page 89. *Look carefully at the IT3 with your helper/ representative. Compare it with any written reasons you have been sent — see above.*

Question 1 asks your boss if he is going to fight the case or not. If he replies "I do not intend to resist the claim", this doesn't mean you automatically win. You still have to go along to the IT hearing and put your case. But obviously you stand a much greater chance of winning when there's no opposition. Unfortunately this is very rare!

Question 4 asks if you were sacked. If he answers "No", then it's likely he is going to say you left of your own accord. You would either have to prove you were sacked or prove "constructive dismissal" (see page 34).

It goes on to ask the reason for sacking you. The answer could be one word, like 'incapability' or "redundancy". See page 39 for substantial reasons for dismissal. It is quite likely he will be able to give one of these here, especially if a solicitor is helping him fill it in. But remember the tribunal still has to decide if this reason was enough in itself to sack you.

Question 5 asks for more details of his case.

Look at the answers to questions 4 and 5 carefully. What do you disagree with? There could be details such as the date you started or finished work, or the amount of your wages. The most important question is whether or not you agree with the reasons given for sacking you. If you do, then you will be fighting the case on the basis that you should not have been sacked for this reason. Your denial of eg misconduct when there is evidence

OTICE OF APPEARANCE BY RESPONDENT   Case Number. 14553/80....

o the Assistant Secretary of the Tribunals
ROIT
43-51 Price Street,
Bristol BS1 4PE.

FOR OFFICIAL USE	
Date of Receipt	Initials

- I *do/do not intend to resist the claim made by Mr H Shaw
- My/Our name is Mr/Mrs/Miss/Title (if a company or organisation):-

Name:	Drainaway Ltd.	
Address:	Bath Street Works,	
	Bath Street,	Telephone Numbe
	Bath,	0225 446400/4

- If a representative is acting for you, please give his name and address and
note that all further communications will be sent to him, not to you:

Name:	Mr H N Plugg - Personnel Manager	
Address:	as above	Telephone Numbe

(a) Was the applicant dismissed?   *YES/NOX

(b) If YES, what was the reason for dismissal?

Unsatisfactory performance of duties

(c) Are the dates given by the applicant as to his period of employment correct?
YYES/NO

(d) If NO, give dates of commencement...5.3.77....and termination...20.5.80.....

(e) Are details of remuneration stated by the applicant correct?   *YES/NOX

(f) If not, or if the applicant has not stated such details, please give the
correct details:-

Basic Wages/Salary:_____ Other Pay or Remuneration:_____

If the claim is resisted, you should give below sufficient particulars to show
the grounds on which you intend to resist the application.
(Continue on reverse if there is insufficient space below).

1. A work rate which did not remotely approach the performance achieved
without undue pressure by drivers employed on similar duties within the
Company.

2. Misuse of company vehicles.

3. Inability to respond to reasonable requests and warnings to improve his
co-operation and attitude to his work.

4. An anomaly in his Driving Licence which could have involved the Company
in legal problems under the Road Transport Acts and which Mr Shaw was not
prepared to correct.

Signature.. Date....15.7.80..............
IT3
(June 1979)   *Delete inappropriate items

against you does not help. Consider whether it will be better to admit it (wholly or in part) and concentrate on arguing that it was quite unreasonable to sack you for it.

If you don't agree with the reason, it's likely you and your boss will be disputing what happened, eg whether your job was redundant or not or whether you did steal stuff from work.

Note For Helpers /Representatives

If you are a helper/representative, the IT3 may be the first information you have about the employer's case. It may be a different story to that told you by the applicant. Don't jump to the conclusion that the applicant hasn't got a case or that she is only telling you half the story. Don't make immediate statements to this effect to her. Remember the employer will be stating his case as strongly as possible, and will omit unfavourable parts. Don't show the feelings you may have about it. They could be wrong. The applicant may lose confidence in you if she thinks you are accepting what her boss says rather than what she says. Don't jump to conclusions. Assess the case slowly and with thought. You can give a frank and considered opinion to the applicant later on. For the moment get her response to the IT3. Do the following:

* Discuss the employer's reply openly with her. Ask her what she thinks of it: is it true? Is it accurate? Get her response to what the employer has said: is she surprised? Or angry? Ask for her replies to what he's written.

* Look at the IT3 with a legal eye. See page 39 on substantial reasons for dismissal. Work out what you have to prove and what the employer has to prove.

IT3 not returned

If your boss does not return the IT3 within 14 days (and has not asked you for further details of your case — see page 54), he will be sent a further letter from ROIT saying the time limit is up. You will be sent a copy of this.

In theory, an employer who does not reply within 14 days can be prevented from defending the case altogther. But in practice an extension of time is always allowed.

90

Further Particulars   **You know a little about your boss's case from letters, forms and the IT3. But it is likely that you do not know many details. You have the right to ask your boss to give you more information about his case.** (rule 4(1) ITRP Regs). Remember, in unfair dismissal cases he has to prove a substantial reason for dismissal and the tribunal will be looking to see if the dismissal was just in all the circumstances. You have the right to know what case you have to answer.

W was dismissed and requested further particulars of the allegations against her. This was refused on the grounds that the onus was on the employer to show that the dismissal was fair and that the proceedings were informal and all the points could be dealt with at the hearing.

The EAT, allowing an appeal by W, held that the particulars should be given so that W could know the details of the case against her and to prepare an answer, thus avoiding the possibility of having to adjourn the hearing.

WHITE v UNIVERSITY OF MANCHESTER. (1976)ICR 419; (1976)ITR 143: EAT.

The further details you can ask for are called "particulars". Strictly speaking, "further particulars" means further than your boss gave on the IT3. **You have the right to know these particulars so that:**
* **you know what case you have to answer.**
* **you know what evidence you have to get for the hearing.**
* **your boss cannot come up with something important and surprising at the hearing.** (You can only *try* to prevent this. The IT can always allow a fresh matter to be brought up if they think it is important).

Writing for further   **To get the particulars you want, write off as soon as**
particulars   **possible to your boss or his representative** (often a solicitor — look in the IT3). **State clearly what details you require and give 7 days for him to supply these.** If you wish, send a copy to ROIT and put a note in your letter to say you have done this. The example letter on page   gives a good idea of what sort of particulars you can ask for. KEEP A COPY OF THIS LETTER.

How should your letter be written? **Your aim should be to tie your boss down to more specific information.**

At the same time, be wary of educating him too much about what you see as weaknesses in his case. Asking for further particulars has two purposes; it provides more information and shows you are not frightened. This can help to get a good settlement. You can worry your boss by asking him for details which may be difficult to provide, and impress him that you are a forceful opponent. Remember that your boss's solicitor may try the same tactic on you; so don't worry or be put off if you receive a heavy letter.

WARNING. This right will not work unless you work to a clearly defined timetable. Don't delay yourself, and beware delaying tactics from your boss or incomplete replies (which are very common). If you estimate there are about 5 weeks to the hearing, then a possible timetable could be:

now: first letter allowing 7 days to reply.

1 week hence: reminder (leave this out if you're short of time).

2 weeks hence: letter to ROIT requesting an order (see below).

3 weeks hence: the further particulars arrive, which leaves you 2 weeks to the hearing.

Employer does not reply satisfactorily – order from the IT

If your boss does not reply, or only gives some of the details you want, you can ask the IT to order him to supply these. The IT has the power (rule4(1)(i) ITRP Regs) to order either party to provide details of their case to the other. Write to the Assistant Secretary to the Tribunal at ROIT, enclosing a copy of the letter to your boss and copy of any reply from him. See the example on page 95.

It is very important to give *full reasons* why you need these details. Your letter will go to a Chairperson of the tribunal, who will decide whether to make the order or not. The Chairperson will only make the order if he thinks your request is justified. He can order all or just part of your request. The order will posted by ROIT to your boss, telling him to give you certain details. You will receive a copy of the order. There is an example on page 96. ROIT usually sends a copy of your letter giving reasons to your boss, so be full yet discrete when you

Example of a combined letter asking for further particulars; discovery and inspection of documents.

H Plugg,
Drainaway Ltd.,
Bath Street,
Bath   25.7.80

Dear Sir,

re: Mr H Shaw, 4 Water Lane, Bristol 6. Case No 14553/80.

I have received a copy of your 'Notice of Appearance' and would be grateful if you would supply me with further particulars of the following statements:

1. "A work rate which did not remotely approach the performance achieved without undue pressure by drivers employed on similar duties within the Company".
Please state:
a) In which way the work is measured. (If _you don't already know_)
b) All facts on which it is intended to rely in support of the allegation that the rate did not remotely approach the performance by drivers on similar duties, including figures relied on.

2. When and by whom warnings were given and the subject matter and terms thereof.
3. "Misuse of Company vehicles".
Please state in what way on what occasions the alleged misuse took place.
4. "Inability to respond to reasonable requests and warnings to improve his co-operation and attitude to his work".
Please state:
a) In what way his co-operation and attitude to work were unsatisfactory; please list.
b) When and by whom any requests for improvement were made.
5. "An anomaly in his driving licence which could have involved the Company in legal problems under the Road Transport Acts and which Mr Shaw was not prepared to correct".
Please state:
a) What the anomaly was. (_if not known_)
b) In what way such an anomaly might have involved a contravention of the provisions of the Road Transport Acts.
c) When and by whom Mr Shaw was asked to correct the alleged anomaly.

(This is the further particulars part of the letter — see page   )

I should also appreciate copies of the following documents:
a) The contract of any written particulars of employment.
b) The disciplinary rules and any grievance procedure.
c) Any notes or memoranda concerning matters of complaint between the parties.
d) Any written warnings.
e) Mr Shaw's delivery sheets for the period 20.3.80 - 20.5.80.
f) Any other written material on which you intend to rely.

(This is the inspection of documents part of the letter — see page   )

Please supply these further particulars and documents within 7 days. I look forward to hearing from you.

Yours faithfully,

write. In some circumstances you could ask ROIT not to send a copy on.

If particulars are still not provided

If your boss still does not provide the information, write to the Assistant Secretary asking for the Chairperson to "strike out" his IT3 or to "debar" him from defending completely (rule4(4) ITRP Regs). See the example on page 97. "Strike out" means in practice that your boss cannot give evidence at the hearing on all or some of the points in his IT3. Eg he says you stole something, but won't supply any details about this, so cannot give evidence that you stole it. So the IT only hears your evidence that you didn't steal anything.

"Debar" means he does not get a chance to speak at the hearing at all, so the IT only hears your evidence. It is very rare for a Chairperson to order this. In addition, either party can be fined up to £100 for not complying with a tribunal order.

You Are Asked For Further Particulars

Your boss can also ask you for further information about your case as described on page 54. Think twice about complying automatically unless it is something you have already alleged in your IT1. Wait and see if the IT order you to supply other particulars. Write to your boss (sending a copy to ROIT) saying it is not reasonable to supply these particulars as:

* he had the chance to ask earlier.
* you have not mentioned them on the IT1.
* in unfair dismissal cases, he has to prove a substantial reason.

   Exceptions to this are:
* if you are saying you were sacked for an automatically unfair reason, eg trade union membership or activities.
* constructive dismissal.
* if your boss says he did not sack you.

In these cases, the onus is on you to prove unfair dismissal, so you may have to provide more information about your case. But remember you are only obliged to disclose relevant and important facts. Refuse other questions.

If you get an order from the IT, then make sure you

Assistant Secretary to the Tribunals,
ROIT,
43-51 Price Street,
Bristol BS1 4PE

Dear Sir/Madam,

      re: Mr Harold Shaw v. Drainaway Ltd. Case No. 14553/80.

    I am the applicant in the above case. I wrote to Mr Plugg, Personnel Manager at Drainaway Ltd on 25.7.80 requesting various further ~~andxbxkker~~ particulars. A copy of that letter is enclosed. I received a reply on 30.7.80 (also enclosed) which made no reference to my requests under no. 1 of my letter, although the response to my other requests were satisfactory. I wrote to Mr Plugg again on 31.7.80 (copy enclosed) stating that I would ask the tribunal for an order if no reply to this request was received by 7.8.80. No such reply was received. Drainaway stated in the IT3 that my work rate was highly unsatisfactory, and this was part of the reason for my dismissal. / time. My request for further   particulars on this point is
I need to know better the case against me and it would also help to save the tribunal's
therefore most relevant, and Drainaway have had ample time in which to provide them.

I therefore request the tribunal to make an order under rule~~tation~~ 4 of the Industrial
                   ure)
Tribunals (Rules of Proced/ Regulations 1980 for the following further ~~andxbatter~~ particulars:

a) In what way drivers' work rates are measured.

b) If the work rate is measured in terms of the number of calls/deliveries made per day - the average number of calls/deliveries made by me and the average number of calls/deliveries made by drivers on similar duties.

c) If my work rate remained constant and if not when it began to deteriorate.

d) The nature of any warnings about my work rate, when and by whom they were made.

Yours faithfully,

Harold Shaw.

Harold Shaw.

Regional Office of the
Industrial Tribunals

43/51 Price Street,
Bristol 1

ORDER OF THE INDUSTRIAL TRIBUNAL

FOR FURTHER PARTICULARS

(Pursuant to Rule 4(1) of the Industrial Tribunals (Rules of Practice) Regulations 198

in the case of

Applicant		Respondent
Harold Shaw	-v-	*Drainaway Ltd*

TO: *H Plugg, Esq.*
Personnel Manager,
Drainaway Ltd.,
Bath Street,
Bath.

Following an application by the applicant for further particulars, a Chairman of

the Tribunals ORDERS that on or before ...*18.8.80*................... you furnish in

writing to .....*Mr H Shaw, 4 Water Lane, Bristol 6* ....

....

....

the following further particulars of the grounds on which you rely and send a

copy to this Office.

1. How drivers' work rates are measured; how the applicant's work rate compares
on average with that of other drivers doing similar duties; and whether the
applicant's work rate has remained constant throughout his period of employment
or has deteriorated.

2. Whether the applicant was warned about his work rate, giving full details.

NOTE:

Failure to comply with this Order may result in the whole or part of your Notice
of Apperance being struck out before or at the hearing.

R Ridgeworth

for Assistant Secretary of the Tribunals

Date: *10.8.80*

cc Mr H Shaw

E03R

Assistant Secretary to the Tribunals,
ROIT,
43-51 Price Street,
Bristol   BS1 4PE.

19.8.80

Dear Sir/Madam,

<u>re: Mr Harold Shaw v Drainaway Ltd, case no. 14553/80.</u>

   I am the applicant in the above case. I am writing to inform you that the
respondents, Drainaway Ltd, have not provided further particulars as ordered
by you on 10.8.80. No reply has been received from them.

   I therefore ask that that part of the 'Notice of Appearance' relating to my
work rate be struck out.

Yours faithfully,

Harold Shaw

Harold Shaw.

give the details ordered. It is vital that you reply promptly and helpfully.

Discovery And Inspection Of Documents

Getting documents from your boss is similar to getting further particulars. You have the right to inspect before the hearing any relevant documents that your boss has. It is better to ask for copies except where:
1. This is not practical, for example details from a whole year's time sheets.
2. The cost of photocopying would be very expensive. (Further particulars don't cost you, but here your boss has a right to ask for payment).

"Discovery" really means finding out what your boss has in his possession on certain topics — what he might be relying on at the hearing. It is not usually very useful. "Inspection" means looking at certain documents, including taking copies. A tribunal cannot make an actual order for copies, although in practice this is the best and most common way of providing inspection.

Documents are relevant if:
* Your boss will produce them at the hearing to help his case.
* They will help your case.

* They have relevance to issues that will come up at the hearing.

What you might want to ask for

You might need to ask for some or all of the following:
— Contract of employment.
— Other written particulars, eg those displayed on the company noticeboard.
— Other documents giving disciplinary and grievance procedures, eg company handbook.
— Any written warnings you are said to have received.
— Documents about your job description, especially if your capability is in question.
— Documents about job structure, promotion prospects, etc.
— Time sheets or clock cards, if relevant.
— Works rules, if relevant.
— Medical notes, if relevant.

- Personnel files or records, including internal notes on your work or behaviour: if misconduct or capability is in question, then any complaints. It is often worth asking to inspect the whole file where this is relevant: if often contains much useful information and gives an opportunity to assess your employer's case and chances.
- Documents concerning investigations into or relating to the events that led up to your being sacked.
- Details of pension scheme, including contributions made by both your boss and yourself, up to the date of dismissal.
- Details of average net earnings, if disputed.
- Copies of any references given.
- Any other written material that your employer may use.

This is not a comprehensive list: ask for *all* documents you require.

How to get these documents

Write to your boss listing what you want to see or have copies of. KEEP A COPY. This could be in the same letter as when you ask for further particulars, but you must make it clear that you are asking for two separate things. See the example on page 93. Give your boss 7 days to supply these, or to give you a date and time to inspect them.

Any inspection will take place either at the workplace or a solicitor's office. You should be given the opportunity to take notes in your own time in a peaceful atmosphere. They may want somebody present: don't be rushed or intimidated by this.

Your boss may reply that he will bring the documents along to the hearing. *This is not good enough. Don't accept this.* Write back saying you want copies/inspection before the hearing, and you will apply for an order if he does not agree to this. As with getting further particulars, you will have to stick to a clear timetable — see page 92.

Order from the IT

If your boss doesn't reply, or doesn't give you all you want, then write to the Assistant Secretary to the

Tribunals at ROIT, enclosing a copy of your first letter to your boss and any reply. Apply for an order to be made under rule 4(1), ITRP Regs. Use the same type of letter as for further particulars – see page 95. Your letter will be put before a Chairperson, who may or may not make the order, depending on whether he thinks the documents are relevant. So always *state the reasons why it is necessary for you to have them.*

If your boss still does not supply the documents he has been ordered to in the time allowed, then write to the Chairperson, via the Assistant Secretary, asking that he be debarred from defending the proceedings or that his notice of appearance be struck out – see page 94.

All documents decided in advance   In some regions, both sides may be asked to tell the tribunal in advance of all the documents they are going to use as evidence and to agree on a numbered bundle for the hearing.

3. CHECKING LAW AND CASE LAW

Introduction   **Case law has become increasingly important. It is a poor reflection on the original aim of Industrial Tribunals, to be simple and accessible, that they have become more and more legalistic.** This has also increased the authority of tribunal Chairpersons and weakened the position of the other two tribunal members. **Case law changes fast; it is important to know recent decisions. Some of the case law we quote in this handbook may be out of date by the time you come to read it.**

Check the law and case law as soon as possible after you have received a copy of the IT3. Don't delay until you have got further particulars, documents, etc.

A law centre or Tribunal Assistance Unit can help you with the legal points and case law relevant to your case. Or you could consider asking a solicitor to advise you through the Green Form scheme – see page 22. Make sure the solicitor is recommended for employment law. Occasionally ACAS will also assist with case law references.

The Law

It is useful to check what the law says about your situation. It may just be general and vague. But at least you know the overall legal framework. Try not to be put off by legal language.

Where to find the law

The employment law with which ITs are concerned is contained in various Acts. See Table 1 on pages 9-16. But most is now gathered together in the Employment Protection (Consolidation) Act 1978 (EPCA). Copies of the Acts can be obtained from HMSO (see Appendix B), Or your reference library should have them. Also, all the Acts are in Hepple & O'Higgins and in Harvey (see nos. 16 and 18, Appendix B), often with explanatory notes. If you can't understand the legal jargon, then look up "Rights at Work", which explains the law in simpler English. The series of DE pamphlets explain different parts of employment protection law, and are fairly easy to read (see Appendix B).

Codes of practice

There are at present 2 codes of practice issued by ACAS, plus the "Industrial Relations Code of Practice" and codes on picketing and the closed shop issued by the DE. These are not law, and an employer is not legally bound to follow them, but they do have some legal standing. The law (s.6(11) EPA) says that the IT shall take into account any code of practice and whether it has been followed. For unfair dismissal ACAS code 1: "Disciplinary practice and procedures in employment" is very important. ACAS code 3: "Time off for trade union duties and activities" deals with the problems to do with dismissal and trade union activities at work. These ACAS codes have replaced sections in the Industrial Relations Code of Practice. But the Industrial Relations code may help you with other problems, eg capability. Details of the codes are included in Appendix B.

Case Law

The decisions of ITs, of EAT, the Court of Appeal (CA), and the House of Lords form "case law". This can be very important. It shows how the law has been understood and put into practice — which is why we have included case law examples throughout this handbook. **These decisions, particularly those made**

by the EAT and higher courts, set precedents. They form a guide for ITs to follow when making their decisions.

Importance of decisions

The only precedents ITs *must* follow are those made by higher courts which interpret unclear bits of law. The rules on the relative importance of decisions are: The most recent decision is the most important: House of Lords decisions are more important than CA decisions; which are more important than EAT decisions; which in turn are more important than IT decisions.

Note that it is only decisions on the law which are binding. Decisions on facts — eg the reasonableness of a decision — are not binding (unless the EAT can say there is only one conclusion which a tribunal properly directing itself could reach, which is a ruling on the law).

How case law helps

Case law can help you in two ways:
1. If you can find a precedent which supports your arguments it is very useful to use at the hearing.
2. To inform yourself of what the other side will be trying to prove. They may be trying to fit the facts of the case in line with a precedent which goes against you. You will need to show that the facts of your case are different and so the IT should ignore that precedent.

Where to find case law

Relevant decisions of ITs, the EAT, and higher courts are reported in:
* Industrial Relations Law Reports (IRLR).
* Industrial Court/Cases Reports (ICR).
* Industrial Tribunal Reports (ITR) no longer being published).
* All England Law Reports (All ER).
* Weekly Law Reports (WLR).
* Queen's Bench Reports.
* IDS Briefs (in summary form only).

You should find these in city libraries, university and polytechnic law libraries, law centres, and some advice centres.

| How to look up case law | We recommend IRLR as the easiest law reports to use from scratch. This is published monthly. It has a good "Casemark" index for finding the case law on the subject you require. |

How to look up
case law

We recommend IRLR as the easiest law reports to use from scratch. This is published monthly. It has a good "Casemark" index for finding the case law on the subject you require.

You can keep up with recent important decisions through IRLR, and "LAG Bulletin" (also monthly), or the IDS "Supplements" and "Briefs". See Appendix B for full details of all these journals.

4. SUPPORTING EVIDENCE AND WITNESSES

Your Own Documentary Evidence

Some of the documents listed in the last section you may have yourself, eg your contract of employment or details of the pension scheme. You may also have other papers which will be useful evidence. For example:
* Letter of notice/dismissal.
* Written warnings.
* Wage slips.
* Jobs applied for/letters of refusal.
* Unemployment benefit forms.
* Medical certificates, if sacked when off sick.
* Your own notes or a diary of the events at work.

Some of these you will need to get, eg a letter from your doctor, or details of sickness benefit received from the DHSS. You must ask for those you don't have straightaway, as it may take some time to obtain replies. Gather all the documentary evidence together.

Witnesses

Is there anyone who could be a witness for you at the IT? For example, was anyone present during the events which led to your dismissal who would support you? Is there anyone who was treated differently to you in the same situation, eg just warned and not sacked? Or someone who has also been treated in a similar bad way by your boss? Is there anyone who could give general evidence about the firm, eg a Health and Safety inspector who was called into the factory, or someone who knows about the unwritten rules of how things are done, which haven't been followed in your case?

Good witnesses can be important and make a big difference to your case, particularly if there is a conflict between what you and your boss are saying. BUT BE VERY CAREFUL WHO YOU CHOOSE AS WITNESSES. Have they been approached by your boss to be witnesses for him? Have they given statements to his representative?

Interview witnesses

You and your helper/representative should see any witnesses as soon as possible. Their memories of vital events may fade. Have a list of questions to ask them. Take notes of what they say. It's vital that you know what a witness will say at the hearing. You must both decide whether they will help your case. They could harm it. Will their evidence be *relevant*? Is it direct knowledge of events, or directly useful to a point in your case? Witnesses failing to stick to the evidence they told you originally is one of the main ways tribunal hearings are lost (sometimes tribunals refer to this as the witness "not coming up to proof"). Will they say things clearly and to the point? How will they stand up to cross-examination? Try to judge whether a witness will really help your case. Make your own judgement on these points.

If your boss has already approached a witness, it is better if he calls her as a witness rather than you. Witnesses *you* call will be expected to be on your side - if they turn out not to be, you cannot challenge their evidence and it will reflect badly on your case.

After meeting the witness, write (or preferably type) **out the evidence she can give.** This is to remind you or your representative so that you know what questions to ask her at the hearing. Write it out in the first person — this makes the events themselves clearer and also makes it easier to decide what questions to ask. There is nothing wrong with giving a copy of this to the witness to help her memory, as it may be a while before the hearing. (But note: a witness is not entitled to have any notes *when* she gives evidence, unless they were made at the time of the event. A tribunal might sometimes allow a memory-aid, but you shouldn't count on it).

If a witness can give evidence on a very important point, eg whether a workmate thumped you first before you defended yourself, **then take a written statement from her.** Write or type out her evidence, and ask her to sign and date it. She will still have to give evidence at the hearing as it is unlikely not to be disputed. The statement is a safeguard, in case she doesn't turn up to the hearing.

WARNING. If she says something different at the hearing, under pressure of cross-examination, she will not be seen as having "come up to proof", which will go against your case.

You could also take a signed written statement from a workmate if you were worried she would say something different at the hearing because she was frightened of the consequences for herself when her boss was present. (In this case do *not* ask her to attend the hearing).

Problems with witnesses

Remember that a witness from your workplace who has not worked for 52 weeks has no protection against unfair dismissal. Make sure she is aware of this. In general, don't ask a witness who has not worked for 52 weeks. She should only be a witness for you if she feels so strongly about you being sacked that she will take the risk. This should be entirely her decision.

Sometimes it is necessary to call a witness even though you know she is not on your side: if the other side won't call her and you need her to give some specific information which only she has. Eg you were off sick and it is alleged that you had no contact with the company over a period. Your evidence is that you called in once a month for wages and talked to Mrs X, the head of wages, and told her your position. If this is the case, let the tribunal know at the beginning exactly why you have to call the witness even though, so far as you are aware, she is not sympathetic.

Witness order

You can compel a witness to come to the hearing by obtaining a witness order (rule 4(1)(b) ITRP Regs). Do this if a witness is reluctant to come voluntarily, or if you're worried about her not turning up, or if the witness is willing to come but wants an order to be able to show her boss that she was forced to go.

Apply in writing to the Assistant Secretary, ROIT, giving the name and home or work address of the witness. State that she is unwilling to attend and give the reasons why her evidence is relevant. See the example on page 107. Your request will be put to a Chairperson who may or may not grant the order. It is unusual for an order not to be granted. ROIT will send the order to you and you have to deliver it to the witness (or send it recorded delivery). There is an example of a witness order on page 108. If a witness does not attend after being ordered, she can be fined up to £100.

In general, *if a witness is not willing to come voluntarily, then you are best not to bother with her.* There can be exceptions to this, eg if she does not want to be involved but her evidence is crucial to the case. Otherwise obtain an order to safeguard the person's position at work, or if she is willing but nervous and you're worried she may not turn up on the day.

Expenses

Witnesses get travel expenses and any loss of earnings up to a limit of (at present) £14 a day. Proof of earnings is not normally required, but the witness has to sign a declaration of what they are. Payment is made by the DE sometime after the hearing. A witness who attends the hearing will normally be paid expenses whether or not she gives evidence. The Chairperson has the right to decide that her evidence, or her attendance, was not necessary, so no payment should be made, but this is very unusual.

Complicated Cases

If a case has become complicated, a "pre-hearing assessment", or "attendance for directions" may be ordered by the tribunal at this stage – see page 113.

18 Horshoe Grove,
Dowlais,
Merthyr Tydfil.
4th September 1980.

Assistant Secretary to the Tribunals,
ROIT,
Caradog House,
1-3 St Andrews Place,
Cardiff CF1 3BE.

Dear Sir/Madam,

re: <u>Ann Barber v Simulated Foam Ltd. Case No. 10714/80.</u>

I wish to request a witness order under rule 4(1) of the Industrial Tribunals
(Rules of Procedure) Regulations 1980 with respect to the above case. The witness,
of 44 Risca Road, Merthyr Tydfil,
<u>Mr John Taylor,</u> is an employee of Simulated Foam Ltd. He was present during the
incident which led to my dismissal, and during the resulting interview in the works
office. His evidence is thus central to my case. He has indicated that he would not
be willing to attend the hearing unless an order is made.

Yours faithfully,

Ann Barber

Ann Barber

CASE NUMBER: 10714/80

Regional Office of the
Industrial Tribunals

Caradog House
....
1-3 St Andrews Place
....
Cardiff CF1 3BE
....

ORDER OF THE INDUSTRIAL TRIBUNAL
FOR ATTENDANCE AS WITNESS

(Pursuant to Rule 4(1)(b) of the Industrial Tribunals (Rules of Procedure)
Regulations 1980)

in the case of

Applicant   Respondent

Ms A Barber   -v-   Simulated Foam Ltd.
....

TO: Mr John Taylor, 44 Risca Road, Merthyr Tydfil.

1.   You are hereby required by ORDER of a Chairman of the Tribunals to attend at
Caradog House 1-3 Andrews Place, Cardiff ....on ....Tuesday, the ...15th

day of ..September........1980 at ..10.00.......am/pm and at any postponed or

adjourned hearing of the proceedings to give evidence.

2.   The Tribunal has power to vary or set aside this Order on the application of
the person to whom it is directed but can only do so for good cause. No such
application can be entertained unless made before the date specified in paragraph
1 of this Order.

NOTE:

Failure to comply with this Order may result in a fine of up to £100 being imposed
upon you under paragraph 1(7) of Schedule 9 to the Employment Protection (Consolidati
Act 1978.

for Assistant Secretary of the Tribunals

Date: 6.9.80

108

5. HEARING DATES

Preliminary Dates   A couple of weeks after you receive a copy of the IT3, you may be sent preliminary dates for the IT hearing. Some ROITs give you a series of dates, usually one week Monday — Friday, during which the hearing will be fixed. They give you a deadline by which to reply and say which dates, if any, are not suitable. There is an example on page 110. If you do not reply it will be assumed all those dates are OK for you. If none of those dates are possible for you, then ROIT will send you a further series of dates, or you can suggest which dates suit you. Your answer to this enquiry is IMPORTANT. Chopping and changing dates later on is very difficult and may be refused.

Date Fixed   Shortly after you reply, or if there has been no preliminary dates enquiry, ROIT will write stating the date, time and place of the IT hearing. They have to give you at least 14 days notice, and usually it is more. There is an example on page 111.

Also enclosed is a letter asking you to send ROIT copies of the documents you will be using at the hearing. This is sometimes advisable but in most regions it is not neccessary.

Postponing The Hearing   A tribunal Chairperson can postpone a hearing at your or your boss's request, but only if you have a good reason. Examples of good reasons are:
* You or your representative or an essential witness could not attend on the proposed date.
* Important documentary evidence (say what and why important) is not yet available.
* You are asked to represent at short notice and it is impossible to prepare the case in time.
* Your boss brings up something new and unexpected in his further particulars reply, and you have to seek other evidence or witnesses.

If a postponement is ordered when it could have been avoided, you or your boss may be ordered to pay the costs of the postponement (rule 11(2) ITRP Regs). For example if you boss gives you documents you have

Regional Office of the Industrial Tribunals
Minerva House 29 East Parade Leeds LS1 5JZ
Listing Section
Telephone 0532 459741

Applicant	Respondent
Mr J Patel	Jackson, Jones and Co. Ltd.

Our reference 24097/80   Date 9th Sept. 1980

It is proposed to list this application for hearing
between ...14/10/80............... and...18/10/80..........
If there are dates in this period which would not suit
you, your representative (if any) or any witnesses, please
return this slip by ...21/9/80.......... If I do not hear
from you by then a date for hearing will be fixed. Once
the date has been fixed postponement will be allowed
<u>only in the most exceptional circumstances</u>.

Generally cases take at least half a day to hear. If
there are circumstances which make you think this case will
take longer please inform me so that arrangements can be
made.

<u>If none of these dates is convenient please advise me of
the reasons AND state when a hearing will be convenient.</u>

S. Clarkson

for Assistant Secretary to the Tribunal

Proposed dates which are
convenient ....

Proposed dates which are
inconvenient ....

Signature .... Respondent/Applicant

Date ....
Case No .....24097/80.....

REGIONAL OFFICE
INDUSTRIAL TRIBUNALS
MINERVA HOUSE
29 EAST PARADE
LEEDS, LS1 5JZ
TEL: 0532 459741

Case No *.74097/80....*

NOTICE IS HEREBY GIVEN THAT THE application of
has been listed for hearing by an Industrial Tribunal at:- 2nd Floor, Minerva House,
29 East Parade, Leeds LS1 5JZ

on *Wednesday,   October 16th   1980*   at *2.00*   am/pm

1.   Attendance should be at the above time and place. The parties (other than a respondent who has not entered an apperance) are entitled to appear at the hearing and to state their case in person or be represented by anyone they wish. A party can choose not to appear and can rely on written representations (which if additional to any already submitted must be sent to the Tribunal and copied to the other party not less than 7 days before the hearing). However, experience shows that it is normally advisable for a party and any witnesses to attend in person even if they have made statements or representations in writing.

2.   It is very important that each party should bring to the hearing any documents that may be relevant, eg a letter of appointment, contract of employment, Working Rule Agreement, pay slips, income tax forms, evidence of unemployment and other social security benefits, wages book, detials of benefits and contributions under any pension or superannuation scheme, etc.

3.   If the complaint is one of unfair dismissal or refusal of permission for a woman employee to return to work after a pregnancy the tribunal may wish to consider whether to make an order for reinstatement or re-engagement. In these cases the respondent should be prepared to give evidence at the hearing as to the availability of the job from which the applicant was dismissed, or helf before absence due to pregnancy, or of comparable or suitable employment and generally as to the practicability of reinstatement or re-engagement of the applicant by the respondent.

4.   If for any reason a party (other than a respondent who has not entered an apperance) does not propose to appear at the hearing, either personally or by representative, he should informe me immediately, in writing, giving the reason and the case number. He should also state whether he wishes the hearing to proceed in his absence, relying on anv written representations he may have made. If an applicant fails to appear at the hearing the tribunal may dismiss or dispose of the application in his absence.

5.   The hearing of this case will take place at the time stated above or as soon thereafter as the tribunal can hear it.

To the Applicant(s) (Ref *Mr S George*   )
    Mr J Patel
    by   *Royal Parks Advice Service,*
          Royal Park Road,
          Leeds 6

Signed ..S. Clarkson.......
for Assistant Secretary of
the Tribunals

Date .... *1.10.80* ....

and the Respondent(s) (Ref *HHB/PI*   )
    Jackson   *Jones & Co Ltd.*
    by   *Phillips, Bridge and Cotton,*
          Eastwardene House,
          233 South Street,
          Leeds 1

NOTE Representatives who receive this notice must inform the party they represent of the date, time and place of the hearing. The party will not be notified direct.

and the Conciliation Officer, Advisory Conciliation and Arbitration Service

111

IT4

not seen just before the hearing, and you ask for a postponement to look through them, the tribunal would probably order costs against your boss (see LADBROKE RACING LTD v HICKEY (1979), IRLR 273: EAT).

How to ask for a
postponement

It is best to try to get the other side to agree to a post-ponement first of all, before you contact ROIT. Then write to ROIT, giving the reasons why you need the postponement and saying the other side is agreeable.

If the other side will not immediately agree, write both to them and to ROIT giving your reason for asking for the postponement.

A postponement may be needed in an emergency, like the day before the hearing because you are ill. Telephone your boss (or his representative) first to try and get his agreement. Then ring ROIT. Do this in the morning if possible, as they can put your request to the Chairperson at lunchtime.

If something crops up on the day of the hearing, like sickness or an accident, make sure someone (eg a friend, relative, union representative or advice centre worker) goes to the hearing, explains what has hap-pened, and asks for a postponement. Tell the other side as they may agree and save bringing their witnesses. If your helper/representative doesn't turn up, don't go ahead with your case. Ask for a postponement. This should be granted if it seems she has a good reason, but the tribunal may well phone her if you have not done so. You might have to pay the costs if she has let you down.

6. PRELIMINARY ISSUES

Preliminary
Hearing

Right at the beginning you will have made a judge-ment as to whether you are eligible to apply. But the question of eligibility may have been brought back as an issue later — your boss may have contested your eligibility in the IT3, or ROIT may have informed you of a problem. For example he may say that you haven't got 52 weeks unbroken employment; or that you were on strike at the time and so can't claim unfair dismissal (s.62 EPCA); or that you are barred from claiming a redundancy payment by your conduct (s.82 EPCA). Now that you have more information from your boss, you are in a much better position to weigh up whether you can convince the tribunal that you are eligible. Any eligibility issues that do exist will be decided either at a "preliminary hearing" (see below), or as a pre-issue at the hearing itself.

A preliminary hearing is ordered if issues can be separated; usually if there is doubt about whether you are eligible to apply to the IT. The preliminary hearing will decide this question only. The idea is to avoid having all the witnesses present, as their evidence won't be necessary if the application is rejected at this stage.

The procedure and rules covering preliminary hearings are exactly the same as for full IT hearings. If the issue is of eligibility, it is up to you to prove that you are eligible, so you will start first. If you are successful at the preliminary hearing, your actual case will be heard at an IT hearing in the usual way.

Preliminary hearings usually take place well before the main IT hearing, but occasionally are booked for the same day — eg if your boss has just one witness and does not want to come to the tribunal twice. In this case you face a full hearing but with the preliminary issue coming up first. Preliminary issues are not always dealt with by a preliminary hearing, however — they may be sprung on you unexpectedly at the hearing itself (see page 130).

Documentary evidence is very important here. In an unfair dismissal case, for example, your wage slips or clock cards can prove that you worked at least 16 hours a week. Get the evidence you need in the usual way — see the sections on further particulars (page 91) and on documentary evidence (page 98).

Pre-Hearing Assessment

Pre-hearing assessments were introduced in October 1980 (rule 6 ITRP Regs), following pre-hearing experiments in Liverpool and Yorkshire. **An assessment only happens in some cases. It is held**

113

when the dispute between the two sides is unclear. It is informal and private usually with an IT Chairperson only. The aim of the assessment is to clarify what the issues are, so that each side knows better what the other is saying and what they have to prove. Also to clarify the case for the tribunal and save time at the hearing.

Quite honestly, I don't think an Industrial Tribunal can help you, after all, WORKING CONDITIONS down here are pretty, well known.

The Chairperson will try and find out what points the two sides agree about and what points are disputed. He will ask if witness orders are required. If you want further particulars, you could state these here. Have them written down for the Chairperson. He can make an order on the spot.

It is possible that the Chairperson could tell you that you have no case. If you then continue to the main hearing, and lost, then costs would probably be

Example of Chairperson's notes of pre-hearing assessment.

Regional Office of the Industrial Tribunals
Minerva House, 29 East Parade, Leeds LS1 5JZ.

Ms P Parker,	Railers Restaurant,	Your reference
Royal Parks Advice Centre,	Buffer Lane,	
Royal Park Road,	Headingley,	Our reference 17280/80
Leeds 6	Leeds 6	Date 11 July 1980

Dear Sir/Madam

MISS C HALL v RAILERS RESTAURANT

The following is the Chairman's record of the pre-hearing assessment of the
above application held on Thursday 7th July 1980.

> The parties were agreeable to give information as requested each to the
> other. The respondents agreed to look at their records and trace a
> former employee called Ann and give the name and address to the applicant.
> The respondents informed the applicant that the wages book would be
> produced at the hearing.
>
> No orders were necessary in respect of witnesses or documents.
>
> The respondent expected to call the proprietor and 2 witnesses to give
> evidence. The applicant would give evidence herself and probably call
> one witness in support.
>
> ACAS is to see the parties at once. The parties agreed that, if settle-
> ment was reached, the tribunal would be informed at once.
>
> The estimate of the time for the hearing was 2 hours. It would seem
> right that this case should be heard at 10.30 in anticipation that it
> may go on longer than that.

This letter is being copied to the Conciliation Officer, Advisory Conciliation
and Arbitration Service.

Yours faithfully

Assistant Secretary to the Tribunals

Copy to: Conciliation Officer

awarded against you (rule 6(2) ITRP Regs). In many cases now, employers ask for a pre-hearing assessment if they think your case is hopeless, to get you warned off.

The aim of the assessment is not to get the two sides to agree to a settlement, although the Chairperson may advise you to consider a settlement through ACAS if he thinks agreement is possible. A few days after the assessment you will receive a copy of the Chairperson's notes. There is an example on page 115.

7. CHECKING OTHER PROBLEMS

Finding Another Job

1. Finding another job. In unfair dismissal cases, the IT can reduce your compensation if they think you have not tried to get another job.

If you get another job before the IT hearing, still carry on with your IT case. But if you win, the compensation will be less than you worked out before. Your loss will be only up to the time you started the new job, plus, if your new wages, perks, etc are less, the difference between your old and new wages, perks, etc for a period of time, eg 6 months or so.

It might be worth trying for a settlement if you find a new job. You and your boss may be more likely to agree if the sum you are asking for is less.

If you don't get another suitable job, remember to keep note of all the jobs you enquire about or apply for.

Unemployment Benefit

2. Unemployment benefit. Earlier (page 58) we referred to the need to fill in the forms the DE sent you carefully and briefly, and to keep a copy of them, including what your boss said. What's happened? Have you had a decision yet from the DE? If your claim for benefit was allowed (you were not disqualified), that's good news. The Insurance Officer at the DE did not think you were sacked for misconduct or left of your own accord. You can refer to this at the IT hearing, although it will not clinch anything as different rules apply.

If you have been disqualified for 6 weeks or less (which is more likely), appeal to a National Insurance Local Tribunal. But ask for the hearing of this appeal not to be set until after the IT, if the Local Tribunal will allow this. When the hearing date of the IT is set, write to the Clerk to the Local Tribunal, informing her.

If the Local Tribunal decides against you, don't despair — they are different decisions on different laws.

8. FINAL PREPARATION

Introduction

This will be different depending on whether you are going to the hearing without help or representation, or representing an applicant, or helping someone to represent themselves, or preparing a case for a Free Representation Unit or other representative. We deal with the different possibilities in turn.

Late Settlement

First, whatever your situation, is there any chance of a late settlement? If you are worried about the hearing or have found out that your case is not as strong as you first thought, it may be worthwhile lowering your bid. Contact your boss or his representative and see if he will consider it. You may be offered a lot less than you want, so be prepared to bargain. But don't settle for much less than you think you would get at the IT. Only settle for a low figure if you feel you will lose. It may be worth mentioning to your boss that his solicitor's bill will be considerably less if there is no hearing, and that if he settles there will be no recoupment by the DHSS/DE (see page 66).

Observation

If you are going by yourself, we strongly advise that you go along to some other IT hearing and observe. There is no problem about this. Just phone to check there is a case on the day of interest to you. You can also ask if there are any cases coming up where the applicant is not represented, so that the hearing you observe will have a similar procedure to yours.

Final Preparation (for helpers/ representatives and applicants representing themselves)

For the hearing you'll need to prepare: an opening statement; your evidence (if you're representing yourself); points to ask your witnesses; points on which to question the other side: and a closing statement.

Opening statement

This should be short. There is no right to make an opening statement, and tribunals will not want to listen to long-winded opening speeches. Decide whether you actually need to give it when the time comes at the hearing – see page 133. Include 3 things:

1. An outline of the issues of the case and what you are trying to prove. For example "My employer alleges I was redundant. I shall show that I was dismissed for union activity and hence was unfairly dismissed".

2. A brief summary of the facts.

3. What witnesses you have and what points they will give evidence on.

If the other side goes first, you can probably omit most of this – see "Who goes first?", page 130.

Your evidence/ written submission

Write down all the points you want to make at the hearing. Make sure you include all relevant facts. You can use this to refresh your memory just before the hearing. You can try taking it to the witness table with you, but the Chairperson may well not allow this. Note also that your helper cannot directly assist you when you give your own evidence.

Alternatively, you can write out a "submission", which you give to the tribunal and to your boss at the hearing. This would include briefly all the main points of your case. You can give more detail at the hearing. The advantage of this is that the tribunal have your evidence before them in writing and you don't need to rely on your memory to say everything you want to. The disadvantages are that your boss's representative has your evidence in front of her at the hearing, which makes it easier to cross-examine you. Also, it is not spontaneous and give rise to a suspicion that it has been prepared with assistance so as to exaggerate the favourable and supress the unfavourable.

Written submissions are probably best where there is a technical matter or line of reasoning to put over and not much dispute over facts. Where it is a question of who the tribunal believe, a written submission cannot really be effective as so much depends on what people's performances have been at the hearing.

A written statement is supposed to be sent to ROIT at least 7 days before the hearing (rule 7(3) ITRP Regs). However, the tribunal will very probably accept a written submission on the day if you are unrepresented.

Questions to your witnesses

Go through the written statements you took from your witnesses. Pick out the points they can give evidence on. Obviously this will not be a complete list for the hearing; you will have to ask other questions at the time.

Prepare yourself and your witnesses for cross-examination by your boss's representative. You or your assistant should think of the awkward points you may be questioned on. What will you reply? What will your witnesses reply?

Questions to your boss's witnesses

You will have to list the points to ask these witnesses at the hearing as they give evidence. But you can prepare a little beforehand. You should have a good idea of the points they will give evidence on and what they will say. Make a list of these points and write down awkward questions to ask.

Closing statement

This can be very important. Again, exactly what you say will depend on what happens at the hearing. But prepare it as much as possible now. See page 136.

Documents

You know what documents you'll need for the hearing. Gather them together. Have you got enough copies? Try to have 6 copies: 3 for the tribunal members, 1 for you, 1 for the other side, and 1 spare.

Preparing An Outline Of The Case For A Representative (for helpers)

The representative should receive your outline ("brief") along with all the documents as much in advance of the hearing as possible. The representative can then read the papers, see the applicant, and do any further preparation.

Exactly when you pass the case on will depend on what you agree with the representative. If you are confident, you may do all the preparation yourself: if not the case could be passed on at an earlier stage.

The outline could include:
* The facts giving all relevant details.
* The employer's case in detail.
* Details of witnesses including their statements.
* Your opinion. This should outline the case to prove, state the strengths and weaknesses of both sides.
* Case law (if you know it).
* A list of all the documents included.

1. INTRODUCTION

How this section is written

This section is for people who are representing themselves, for helpers who assist the applicant at the hearing without being a fully-fledged representative, and for representatives. We suggested that trade unionists and advice centre workers might want to act as helpers rather than as representatives (see page 4). But if you are more experienced with IT cases, then go ahead and be a full representative.

This section is about the actual tribunal hearing. What happens at the hearing? Who will be there? How formal will it be?

Legal structure

Rules for tribunal procedure are laid down in the Industrial Tribunal (Rules of Procedure) Regulations 1980 (ITRP Regs). These give basic information about how the tribunal should be conducted and about the rights and responsibilities of both sides.

How formal is it?

ITs are supposed to have an "easily accessible, speedy, informal and inexpensive procedure" for the ordinary person (Donovan Royal Commission, 1968). They are supposed to "avoid formality" (rule 8(1) ITRP Regs). But they are a lot more formal than other sorts of tribunal. No one wears wigs or gowns but they are still more like a court. You may be expected to stand up when the tribunal members come in or go out, and you swear an oath when you give evidence. There are rules of procedure and evidence. These rules are quite strict when both sides have representatives, but relaxed when applicant or employer are representing themselves. Some allowance is usually made for inexperienced representatives. How formal the hearing will be differs from area to area and from Chairperson to Chairperson — tribunals have the power to arrange the procedure largely as they wish (rule 8(1) ITRP Regs). With the passage of time they have become more formal — an invasion of lawyers has brought increased legalism.

2. WHO IS AT THE HEARING

The Chairperson

The Chairperson. We use "Chairperson" in this handbook, but virtually all are men. In 1978 there were 72 full-time and 133 part-time Chairpersons in England and Wales, and only 6 were women. They are all solicitors or barristers with at least 7 years qualified experience, though their training does not need to be in employment law. They are appointed by the Lord Chancellor. Full-time Chairpersons are at present paid £17,250 per year; part-time Chairpersons £75 per day. The Chairperson takes charge of the hearing and asks most of the questions. He should make careful note of all relevant evidence given to the tribunal. He takes a very prominent part in the proceedings, while the other two members usually take little part in the hearing itself, though they may play more part in the discussions afterwards.

The Chairperson will usually assist unrepresented applicants by questioning the employer's witnesses, bringing out inconsistencies, weaknesses, etc. He should question fully and help the unrepresented applicant and her witnesses when they give their evidence, to bring out all the relevant points of the applicant's case.

The Two Other Members Of The Tribunal

The other two members. These are members of management and of trade unions. They are chosen by the Secretary of State for Employment from panels submitted by the CBI and TUC and other bodies representing employers and employees. About 20% are women. They are paid £30 per day.

The Clerk

The Clerk. Your tribunal will have its own Clerk. Her jobs are:
* to meet you on arrival.
* to explain to you about the tribunal hearing.
* to answer any queries you may have.
* to deal with expenses claims.
* to assist administratively with the running of the hearing.
* to find case law for the tribunal.

Her duties are only administrative — she takes no part in the decision-making.

The Public

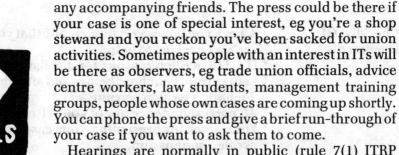

The Public. ITs are open to the public. But usually there's no-one else there apart from the two sides and any accompanying friends. The press could be there if your case is one of special interest, eg you're a shop steward and you reckon you've been sacked for union activities. Sometimes people with an interest in ITs will be there as observers, eg trade union officials, advice centre workers, law students, management training groups, people whose own cases are coming up shortly. You can phone the press and give a brief run-through of your case if you want to ask them to come.

Hearings are normally in public (rule 7(1) ITRP Regs). Private hearings can be allowed in limited circumstances, but are very rare.

Witnesses

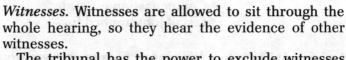

Witnesses. Witnesses are allowed to sit through the whole hearing, so they hear the evidence of other witnesses.

The tribunal has the power to exclude witnesses from the hearing. You may not want the other side's witnesses to be present during your evidence or to hear what other witnesses on that side say. This could be important if there is a serious conflict of evidence between what you say and what the other side will say.

Or you may believe that a witness for your boss is going to untruthfully back up her evidence. Request to the Chairperson either that the witness be excluded from hearing the evidence of other witnesses, or that all witnesses on both sides wait outside before giving evidence. You must give good reasons why this is important, as the Chairperson will be reluctant to do it. Make your request at the very beginning of the hearing.

It is virtually unknown for witnesses to be excluded. The authors of this handbook consider this one of the most unsatisfactory features of ITs. Cases very often turn on a conflict of fact when respondent (and applicant) are allowed to have corroborative witnesses present, thus robbing the other side of any real opportunity to properly test the strength of the evidence

3. ARRIVING AT THE HEARING

Checklist Of Documents

Check you have everything ready that you will need. Here's a checklist to help:
* IT1, IT3, written reasons for dismissal, DE forms.
* Letters from your boss before and after the dismissal, including written warnings.
* All correspondence about your IT case.
* Your notes for presenting your case, including any written submission.
* Witness statements.
* All documents to be used as evidence.
* Relevant case law and relevant Acts.
* Compensation estimate.
* List of jobs applied for.

Arriving At The Hearing

It's a good idea to arrive early to sort out any last minute details with witnesses, etc. Arrange to meet 30 minutes beforehand. Make your way to the waiting room for applicants. There is another separate waiting room (called "Respondents") for your boss and his representative and witnesses. Any other people in the same waiting room as you will be other applicants, so don't worry about them hearing your conversation.

There should be a noticeboard somewhere near your waiting room to show you which room your case is being heard in, and who the members of your tribunal are. (If you find you know one of the members, you may want to tell the Chairperson, who will arrange for a new member to replace that one, or postpone the hearing. Or you can carry on, if both sides agree, with the Chairperson and the remaining member).

The clerk will ask your name and whether you are represented and how many witnesses you have. Make clear to her the role of your helper. Tell her that your helper is just a friend who has come along to help, and not a representative. The Clerk may ask how long you think the case will last. Normally a case will last the whole day if there is more than just you and your boss giving evidence. She'll ask if you have any documentary evidence, and usually make copies of any documents if you haven't already done so. Let her have a list of any cases you are going to refer to, and where the references to them are to be found, so she can get them for the tribunal from the library.

Expenses

Ask the Clerk about expenses and loss of earnings (see page 106). Usually you won't get them until after you have given evidence. She will then give you a form to fill in. You don't get cash on the spot, but will be sent a cheque. When you (or your witnesses) claim loss of wages, your present boss does not normally have to sign the form, but the tribunal may contact him directly for confirmation.

In The Waiting Room

Go over the evidence

Go over the evidence you will give by looking through your statement. Your helper should do the same thing with your witnesses. This refreshes everyone's memory. You cannot normally have any notes when you give evidence (see page 104).

What are the important points you need to prepare your witnesses for for the approaching hearing? Tell your witnesses they should direct their attention and speak to the Chairperson when giving evidence. Tell

them that the Chairperson will be taking notes and that they should WATCH HIS PEN and not go too fast. Warn them to speak slowly in short sentences and not a long ramble, and to wait while he is writing. This is very important. The Chairperson will only note down what he can and might miss some important fact if they go too fast. The more they ramble or speak inaudibly the less the tribunal will take notice.

Warn about cross-examination

In cross-examination by the boss's representative, tell witnesses to answer briefly where possible. They often only have to say "yes" or "no". If they stay silent, it will be a point against them. Sometimes it is important to answer more fully, eg if the other side is trying to get them to agree to something to the boss's advantage. Eg: "You were late every morning that week, weren't you?" "Yes, *but* I made up the time by taking a short lunch break".

Give reassurance (for helpers/ representatives

The applicant and any witnesses may be nervous. Reassure them that they have nothing to worry about. It's not like a criminal court. No one is on trial. The tribunal should be quite friendly to both sides. Explain that they will swear on oath, but they will give their evidence sitting at a table, not from a court-like witness box. (If someone isn't a Christian, check beforehand what alternatives to swearing they have).

Last-Minute Settlement

On arrival at the hearing, you or the other side can approach each other about a possible settlement (or other matters, eg agreeing on a numbered bundle of documents). If you are discussing a settlement, ask the Clerk to inform the tribunal what is happening. They will normally agree to postpone the start of the hearing whilst you negotiate. You may have to talk in one of the two waiting rooms, as there may be no private room. If you can't agree, tell the Clerk you're ready to start the hearing. You do not have to give the tribunal any details of your negotiations.

Wording of any settlement

If you agree on a settlement, be careful about the wording of the agreement. See page 75 and the

126

example on page 83. Write it out yourself at the time on a bit of paper. It must be signed by both sides. If a reference is part of the settlement, ask the other side to write out the wording of that *now* before you sign. If the reference is not satisfactory, ask for it to be amended as you want it.

Informing the IT

Go into the tribunal and inform them of your agreement. Show them the signed agreement (though you don't have to tell them what the settlement is). Tell them the deadline for the settlement to be put into effect (ie 14 or 28 days). *Ask them to "adjourn the case generally until further order". This is important.* If you don't request an adjournment, the IT decision will state "in full and final settlement" and you will not have the option to re-open the case if your boss doesn't keep to the settlement. The IT will send you a written decision.

Tribunal Member Not Present

If one of the tribunal members is not present and a replacement cannot be obtained, then your case will be postponed to a later date, unless everyone agrees to a hearing with two members (the Chairperson has a deciding vote). (ITRP Regs rule 9(1)).

Witness/Helper Representative/ Applicant Doesn't Turn Up

If someone doesn't turn up and you don't know any reason why, tell the tribunal and try and get enquiries made. ASK FOR THE START OF THE HEARING TO BE POSTPONED in case they are just late. If they don't arrive, ask for an adjournment unless they are not crucial to your case. Try and *find out the reason why they haven't come,* so you can inform the tribunal requesting an adjournment. However, the tribunal may think it is your job to have witnesses there and carry on anyway.

127

4. AT THE HEARING

Going into
the hearing

The Clerk will show you to the tribunal room, and you and you helper/representative sit at the table for applicants next to each other. The other side will sit at the table next to yours. Depending on the region, the tribunal may or may not be there. If not, they will make their entrance soon and you will be asked by the Clerk to stand up! A ridiculous formality for a supposedly informal hearing.

Role Of Helpers
(for helpers)

As a helper you won't be able to speak for the applicant at the hearing. However, the applicant should feel free to ask the Chairperson for a few minutes to consult with her helper when necessary. There has to be an understanding between you and the applicant about how you are going to communicate with each other: by written note, whispering in her ear, tapping on the shoulder to indicate that the applicant should ask for a brief break to consult, etc. Remember you are helping the applicant to help herself, and too many breaks may put the applicant out of her stride.

You sit beside the applicant and take notes of questions to and answers from all witnesses. The notes are useful for reference back to what a witness said.

When the other side
is giving evidence

When the other side is giving evidence, take special note of:
* points made against the applicant.
* points where their version differs from the applicant's
* points the applicant contests.
* weaknesses in their evidence.

Write down questions which the applicant should ask their witnesses in cross-examination.

When the applicant
is giving evidence

When the applicant is at the witness table, note if there are any points she has forgotten to mention. See her statement or written submission. If she omits a point, you could try saying to the tribunal that she wished to give evidence on such-and-such a matter.

Keep your interruptions to a minimum or get the applicant to ask for a few moments to consult over difficult points.

When the applicant is being cross-examined

When she is being cross-examined, note:
* any admissions by her that favour the other side.
* If they confuse her and she gives the wrong answer. There should be an opportunity for her to correct later after cross-examination, in what is known as re-examination.

When your witnesses are giving evidence

When your witnesses are giving evidence, have their statements and list of questions to ask them at hand. Make sure all the questions are asked and all points covered. You won't be able to bring up anything *new* in re-examination.

Closing statement

Help with the closing statement by listing the main points in the applicant's favour and the other side's weaknesses. See page 136.

Note For Applicants (for applicants)

If you are REPRESENTED, remember that the tribunal normally expect that everything goes through your representative. She is your voice, except when you are giving evidence at the witness table. One exception might be if you have specialist knowledge you could use in cross-examination of the other side — eg technical points, or knowledge of factory layout. Obviously you will have a closer knowledge of the facts of your case than your representative, so you will be able to look for points your representative misses. Read the section above to see what sort of points to look for.

What Happens?

The Chairperson may introduce himself and the other tribunal members. He may ask you if you are representing yourself. You may need to clarify the role of your helper. He should outline the order of events. He'll say who goes first and presents their case. He'll tell you about your right to question the other side's witnesses (cross-examine). He may offer to help out in cross-examining.

Don't feel you have to swept along by the tribunal. If you need to gather your thoughts, note down points,

129

have a talk with your helper, look something up, etc; then ask the tribunal if you could have a few moments for this purpose. ITs are quite slow moving and such a request is quite in order.

Preliminary Issues   Sometimes you will know that the first thing to be covered at the hearing is a preliminary issue, where you will have to go first: eg you have to prove that you have worked for an unbroken period of 52 weeks. Sometimes, however, the preliminary issue may come as a surprise to you. This is one of the main snags that may come up at the beginning of the hearing. If you have prepared the case properly you will have looked out for any possible preliminary issue — see page 112. Don't get caught by surprise. If necessary, ask for a short adjournment to look up the law or think about what to say. Make sure you have got it clear what the other side think.

Who Goes First?   The IT controls procedure at the hearing, and occasionally will change the order of events from what you expect. But normally **who goes first depends on who has to prove the case. In unfair dismissal cases, a dismissal is quite often admitted and so it is up to your boss to prove a substantial reason, so he goes first. But there are exceptions. The burden of proof is yours, and you go first, in the following cases:**
1. Your boss says he didn't sack you, but you left of your own accord. It is up to you to prove that you were sacked. If you win this part then your boss will have to prove that sacking you was fair.
2. In constructive dismissal cases you have to prove that the behaviour of management forced you to leave — see page 34.
3. If you say you were sacked for trade union membership and/or activites, before you worked for 52 weeks.
4. You were sacked during a strike or lock-out, and other workers were not, or you were not taken back on when others were — see page 44.

Redundancy cases, where you dispute there was a genuine redundancy situation, are like normal unfair dismissal cases. Your boss has first to prove that the reason for sacking you was redundancy (ie a substantail reason). So he starts.

Model Procedure   **The side that goes first gives their evidence, calls all their witnesses in turn (if any), and completes their case. The other side is restricted to cross-examination. Then the other side goes through their evidence. We outline the order things happen when the employer goes first.**

1. **Employer's opening statement** (optional).
2. **Employer's witnesses:** – evidence in chief
        – cross-examination by you
        – re-examination by the
           employer
        – questions from the
           tribunal (at any stage)
3. **Your opening statement** (optional).
4. **Your witnesses:** – evidence in chief
        – cross-examination by the
          employer
        – re-examination by you
        – questions from the
          tribunal (at any stage)

5. **Your closing statement.**
6. **Employer's closing statement.**
Never assume a fixed order, because if you have made a mistake about some point (eg a preliminary issue) you could end up going first anyway. Prepare your case flexibly.

Employer's   If your boss goes first, his opening statement is likely
Opening Statement to be longer than yours. It *could* contain the following:
* an outline of the facts, eg when you started work, what happened, and disciplinary warnings, when you were sacked.
* an outline of what he has to prove. So if dismissal was for abuse to management, that this was a substantial reason, and dismissal was reasonable in the circumstances.
* the witnesses he will call and what points they will give evidence on.

Employer's Witnesses

* a background of the company, its size, hierarchy, the sort of work it does.

If everything is plain from the IT3 and IT1, however, his statement may be much shorter or left out altogther.

Note down what is said, particularly his version of the facts. You may want to dispute some of these. Don't interrupt now. You can do this in your opening statement later on.

Evidence in chief

Your boss's representative will take your boss and other witnesses through their evidence by asking them questions. Make sure their witnesses do not have notes with them at the witness table. If they do, *object* to the Chairperson. The witnesses will give their version of things and may be asked questions about things you said on the IT1. (Remember the problem mentioned on page 123 on the rarity of excluding witnesses).

Take careful note of all points you dispute, and of everything said against you. You will need to question their witnesses about the points you dispute and give your version of events when you give your evidence.

Cross-examination

Use the list of points you prepared before (see page 120), plus what you have just noted down from their evidence, plus any suggested questions from your helper. You can ask them about things they have covered in their evidence and other matters *which they have not mentioned but which you will be bringing up when you give your evidence.* If you don't ask them about these matters now, you may be criticized for not having put them when you give your evidence. This is because the witnesses may have to be brought back to deal with these points. Don't worry about being slow to ask questions. Don't rush on to your next question without having thought what you want to say.

WARNING. As much as possible, don't ask questions if you don't know what they will reply. It could work against you. Eg: "You said that I upset other staff. Well, in what way did I upset other staff?" The answer could well be a list of incidents which you wish had not been mentioned. Similarly, don't ask a lot of questions just because it looks good or you think you should.

In cross-examination, you can also make statements of your version and ask the witness if she agrees: "Isn't it right that......?" You can also do this to counter a point she made in her main evidence: "You said....., but wasn't it the case that ......?" You may want to do this about your boss's reply to your IT1. If you have evidence of your boss saying contradictory things in documents be sure to tune in on this.

If there is a direct conflict between your version and his, you can state your version and ask the witness "Is that not so?" Eg: "I put it to you that ......If the witness answers no, that's OK. The tribunal are aware of the conflict of evidence, and it's to them who they believe. If the witness does not reply at all, that helps your case – don't ask again.

If evidence from the other side is untrue, it is very important to challenge it. don't let it go by and hope to deal with it later.

Tribunal's questions	Questions from the tribunal can come at any stage, but usually there is a special space for a block of questions at this stage. The Chairperson is likely to ask his questions first, and then ask the other two members if they have any. In some regions he may ask his questions after the other members' questions.
Re-examination	Your boss's representative now has the chance ot ask his witnesses further questions, but only on the points raised so far. She shouldn't ask questions about new matters.

If a new matter *is* raised in re-examination however, you should also be asked if you have any further questions.

THIS IS THE PROCEDURE FOR *EACH* OF THEIR WITNESSES. ALL OF THEIR WITNESSES WILL GIVE EVIDENCE BEFORE YOU PUT YOUR CASE.

Your Opening Statement	This can usually be brief or left out when the other side has already put their case. Your cross-examination should already have given a good idea of points you are relying on. Include the following:

* any dispute over the main facts they gave in their opening statement which is not obvious already.

* you've heard your boss's case, so inform the tribunal what main points you agree with and what you dispute.
* briefly outline what you will be trying to prove.

Your Evidence

It is normally expected that you give your evidence first, and then evidence from any witnesses you have. You may want to give out a written submission of all your main points — see page 118. Give copies of this to all, including the other side. The advantage of a written submission is that your evidence is there before the tribunal. You can take a copy of it to the witness table, as it has been made available to all. You can either expand on the points made in it, or just let the Chairperson ask you questions.

If you don't have a written submission, the Chairperson will ask you to tell the tribunal in your own words exactly what happened. He will start off by asking you questions. But it will be up to you to state your view on matters he doesn't ask you about. This relies on your memory, plus assistance from your helper.

You will no doubt want to make additional points now you have heard the other side's evidence. Ask the Chairperson if you can take notes of their evidence with you to the witness table, as you wish to dispute certain matters. Otherwise you will have to rely on memory. Your helper should assist by saying to the tribunal that you wanted to give evidence on such-and-such a point.

When the Chairperson finishes questioning you, you have the chance to state anything further you wish to; for example you view on points from the other side's evidence.

Tips

Here are some tips to help you:
* Don't go off into a long irrelevant ramble. Stick to the important points and be brief. Speak clearly: the strongest case in the world can be ruined by mumbling!
* Don't be surprised if the Chairperson frequently interrupts you or asks you to repeat things. He has to make a note of all the main points of your case. GO SLOWLY AND WATCH HIS PEN.

* Date and time sequences are very important. Before the hearing, make sure you know all the exact dates, or approximate dates if it is a while ago. Don't jump backwards and forwards in time: give your evidence in the right time order.

THIS IS YOUR CHANCE TO STATE YOUR CASE. HAVE YOU SAID EVERYTHING THAT YOU WANTED TO? HAVE YOU OMITTED ANY POINTS THAT SUPPORT YOU?

Cross-examination
You will now be questioned by your boss's representative. Be careful with your answers. She will be trying to force you into replies that don't help your case. In general just answer "yes" or "no". And only answer the question that you are asked. Don't go on about anything else. See page 126.

Your boss's representative can also "put" things to you. She will make statements of your boss's version and ask you: "Is that not so?" Reply firmly: "No, that's incorrect" if you disagree. Or "Yes, except that ....." Do not stay silent.

Questions from the tribunal
Give full replies to their questions.

You now have the right to amplify or correct any points on which you have been cross-examined. Ask for a few moments to get your bearings or jot points down if you need to. You can't bring up any new matters. But you may want to restate your view on matters that went badly for you in cross-examination. Or you may want to emphasise the strong points in your case. But be brief. If you repeat too much the tribunal may get irritated.

Your Witnesses
You may be asked what issues your witnesses can tell the tribunal about.

Evidence in chief
You can either question your witnesses or you can ask the Chairperson to do it, or a combination of both. If you feel stuck at this point you can always ask the Chairperson to do the questioning. But it is better to do it yourself — you know best what the witnesses can say.

Be careful not to ask questions on irrelevant points. Make sure your questions are specific to the important

135

issues and on points that are disputed by your boss. Do not ask leading questions on matters that may be disputed. So it is fine to ask: "Do you live at 66 Ash Grove, Carlisle?". But you might be told off if you asked the more contentious: "Did he then call you a bastard and hit you on the jaw with his fist?". If the answer is put into the witness's mouth like this it loses its effect on the tribunal. So instead ask: "Did he say something?" "What did he do next?".

If your witness is going too fast for the Chairperson to note it all down, tell her to stop and watch his pen. You can do this periodically. When asking your questions, wait until he's finished writing before asking the next.

Include all questions you want to ask now, as you cannot ask questions on new points in re-examination.

Cross-examination   Take careful note of your witnesses' replies to cross-examination. If they are forced into saying something which goes against you, note this down.

Re-examination   You can try and remedy the situation by questioning them again on these points, hoping for a more favourable reply.

Your Closing Statement

If the other side went first, then they finish last. You make the first closing statement. This statement can be very important. You want to remind the tribunal of the main points of your case. Much of what you say will be repetition. That's OK, as long as you are brief. You could:

1. repeat what you are trying to prove.

2. remind the tribunal of evidence given by witnesses and of documentary evidence in your favour. Don't misrepresent what was said in evidence — eg if one of your witnesses did not say what you thought she was going to say when you prepared your case.

3. state the strong points of your case; eg

— disciplinary procedure at odds with the code of practice.

— you were not given a chance to explain your side of things.

— other workers were treated differently.

— the employer should have taken alternative action to dismissal.
4. answer points made against you; eg
   — you were not able to do the job well because you were not given enough training.
   — your misconduct was not misconduct, but your boss's unreasonableness.
5. state the main weaknesses of your boss's case; eg
   — contradictions in his evidence.
   inconsistencies in his reasons for dismissal.
6. give reasons why your version should be preferred, if there is a conflict of evidence.
7. refer to relevant law and case law if you feel able to do so.

Prepare at least an outline of your closing statement before the hearing, but be ready to add or change points at the time.

Don't be upset if the Chairperson starts discussing the case with you. He may dismiss certain topics because the tribunal all think that clearly things are in your favour on them. If he points out difficulties, he is not being hostile, he is letting you know what troubles the tribunal and it is here that you have your chance to persuade the tribunal in your favour.

Employer's Closing Statement

Your boss's representative will now make her closing statement.

The tribunal will then go out of the room to consider all the evidence and to make their decision. (Both sides may be asked to retire to their waiting rooms). This will usually take at least 20 minutes, and quite likely longer. You can go out for a smoke or a break if you wish, but be nearby so the Clerk can find you if the tribunal return quickly.

Adjourning Part Heard

If your boss brings up new points against you during the hearing that he hasn't mentioned before, then consider asking for an adjournment. Eg he states a different reason for dismissing you, or presents as evidence a personal file you didn't know about despite having asked him writing. Ask for the hearing to be adjourned for a short time (30 minutes) for you to consider the new evidence. (Don't assume this will always be allowed). If you need to bring other witnesses or get other documentary evidence to answer these new points, then ask for an adjournment to a later date. The tribunal should be favourable to this if it was something you couldn't foresee, especially if you have already asked for further particulars and documentary evidence.

Expenses

Remember to see the Clerk about expenses after you and your witnesses have given evidence. Representatives who are unpaid (eg volunteer advice workers) should also receive expenses.

Note if there is more than one applicant

If there is more than one applicant in the same case, you have a choice about how you put your case. Either all the applicants can go to the witness table in succession, with their witnesses after they've all finished, or the first applicant can give evidence followed by her witnesses, then the next applicant and hers. The choice will depend on the case.

5. THE DECISION

How The Decision Is Given

The tribunal will return and give you their verbal decision there and then. LISTEN CAREFULLY, OR YOU MAY MISS IT. The Chairperson will often speak into a microphone to tape record the decision and reasons, and will not address himself to you. **The decision will often be stated rapidly right at the beginning,** straight after he's said the case number and the names of you and your boss. For example:

"Case number ....

Vera Smith v J Brown and Co. Ltd.

The unanimous decision of the tribunal is that the applicant was unfairly dismissed".

He will continue by giving a summary of the evidence and the reasons for the decision. The decision may be stated again at the end. If your case involves a section 53 claim, or other claim, as well, then listen for two or more decisions.

138

Contributory fault

If the decision is that you were unfairly dismissed, **the tribunal will also state whether you were partly to blame; ie whether you "contributed" to your own dismissal.** If so, they should estimate any contribution as a percentage; ie 50% contribution means you were unfairly dismissed, but that you were as much to blame for the events as your boss.

'Obsolescence is the name of the game here Hemmings, this thing will last for years — we're firing you for INCOMPETENCE'

At the beginning of the tape recording, the Chairperson should merely state whether you were unfairly dismissed or not. But listen carefully as he may say later on that you contributed to the dismissal. He may or may not give the exact percentage contribution.

After this part of the decision, the tribunal will go on to talk with you and your boss about compensation, reinstatement or re-engagement. (Exceptionally he might have asked you to deal with these topics before, but the proceedings are nearly always split up so the question of blame is decided first, and then compensation, etc, only if necessary afterwards).

Delay in decision

Occasionally, if the case is complex, or has been a long one, or it is getting late, or the tribunal members are divided in their opinions, they will not be able to give you a decision there and then. The decision is

139

called a "reserved decision", and reasons will be sent to you by post after a few weeks.

Written decision

You will not receive a decision in writing on the day. But you will be sent a written reasoned decision by ROIT around 2–3 weeks later. There is an example on pages 151-154.

If the decision is against you, then that's the end of your IT case. But you can consider asking for a review or appealing higher. See pages 156 and 157.

Remedies

If the decision is in your favour, then the next question is whether you get your job back or compensation. You will have already written on the IT1 whether you want reinstatement or compensation. But you can change your mind. If you want reinstatement or re-engagement, but did not put this on the IT1, it would have been best to have informed ROIT and your boss in writing at least 7 days before the hearing (rule 11(3) ITRP Regs). But if you didn't, the tribunal should still ask you at the hearing.

Reinstatement

Reinstatement is defined on page 50.

If you have not found another job, the tribunal must ask you whether you want your old job back (s.68(1)

'I'd have preferred REINSTATEMENT as a keeper, but I suppose this is better than nothing'

EPCA). If you do, they will then ask your boss whether he is willing to take you back. If he isn't, you should both get a chance to state your reasons, and the tribunal will decide whether or not reinstatement is "just" and practicable. His reasons could be that your job has been filled or that you were partly to blame for the dismissal. Your boss (and his witnesses) will have to give evidence, and you can cross-examine him about his reasons.

What the tribunal must consider

In deciding whether to order reinstatement, the tribunal has to consider, in order of importance (s.68(1), 69(5) EPCA):
1. your wishes.
2. whether it is practicable for your boss.
3. when you were partly to blame for the dismissal, whether reinstatement would be "just".

Your wishes should be given much more weight than the desires or convenience of your boss.

Not practicable would be a SERIOUS risk of industrial action if you returned, or a SERIOUS risk of conflict with your supervisors (COLEMAN v MAGNET JOINERY. (1975)ICR 46:CA). For example, the fact that your boss has taken on a permanent replacement to do your job should only concern the tribunal if he can show that it was impossible for the work to be done without a permanent replacement (s.70(1) EPCA). (This assumes you put reinstatement on your IT1. If you didn't, your boss was justified in replacing you). Arguments from your boss like you don't get on with management or your return to work would undermine their authority should be ignored by the tribunal. *But* if you worked for a very small firm, it not likely that reinstatement would be forced on an unwilling employer except in exceptional circumstances (ENESSY CO. S.A t/a THE TULCHAN ESTATE v MINOPRIO. (1978)IRLR 489: EAT).

If you were partly to blame for the dismissal, the tribunal decides if reinstatement would be "just". This depends a lot on the extent you contributed to your own dismissal. Your contributory fault affects the decision whether or not to order reinstatement, but once rein-

141

statement is ordered, the contribution cannot affect the terms. Reinstatement cannot have a punitive element (see page 50).

Arguing your case   If you want reinstatement, be ready to argue your case. If your boss says that it is not practicable, he has to prove that. Cross-examine him about his reasons. Eg, if he has taken on a permanent replacement:
* couldn't existing staff have covered your work?
* what would have happened if you had been off sick for a few weeks?
* couldn't he have taken on a temporary replacement?
* he knew you wanted your job back, didn't he?

Let the tribunal know you are aware of the law about reinstatement. In conclusion, state that your wishes should be given priority, and that your boss has not proved that it is impracticable for him to take you back. The tribunal will decide if reinstatement is just. If they decide it is not, they should then consider re-engagement.

Re-engagement   **If the tribunal decides that it is impracticable or unjust for you to get your old job back, then you could ask for another vacancy at your old firm or in an associated company.** This means a company under the same ownership; eg you firm might be a subsidiary of another or a member of a large group of companies. The other job should be "comparable and suitable". "Comparable" means the same sort of work and the same pay. "Suitable" means personally suitable to you; eg taking into account the distance you would have to travel to work. Question your boss about other vacancies. He should give detailed information about these, provided that you gave at least 7 days notice before the hearing of wanting reinstatement or re-engagement (rule 11(3) ITRP Regs). If he cannot answer satisfactorily, eg he does not know about vacancies in associated firms, then ask for an adjournment. The tribunal can order your boss to pay the costs of a further hearing.

Re-engagement can also mean that you get your old job back, but without any arrears of pay for the period

142

between dismissal and your return to work. This could happen if the tribunal decided you were partly to blame for your dismissal, and did not consider reinstatement to be just in the circumstances (see above). Re-engagement *can* have a punitive element if you were partly to blame for your dismissal – see page 50.

Decision Of Reinstatement Or Re-engagement

If the tribunal orders reinstatement or re-engagement, it should specify clearly on the written decision:
* the name of the employer (if re-engaged by an associated firm).
* the nature of the job (if re-engaged by an associated firm).
* the rate of pay (if re-engaged by an associated firm).
* the amount of money payable to you for loss of wages, including overtime.
* any rights and privileges which must be restored, such as pension rights or company car.
* the date the order must be put into effect.

Is a decision of reinstatement/re-engagement likely?

Only about 2% of unfair dismissal applications result in reinstatement, even though this is supposed to be the first aim of the IT when there is unfair dismissal. Even though tribunals are forced to consider reinstatement before any other solution, they actually order it very rarely – indeed the chances of reinstatement or re-engagement are about 3 times greater through a settlement than through an IT hearing. Reinstatement is the only chance an unfairly sacked person has of getting her job back; despite its importance, it is ordered appallingly seldom.

To be fair to tribunals, this is very often because applicants don't ask for reinstatement. Helpers and representatives should ensure that discussion on this is thorough, and point out that compensation can often be a short sighted remedy and reinstatement be more suitable, especially in the present economic climate.

Compensation

If you do not want reinstatement or re-engagement, or the tribunal decide not to order this, they then consider how much compensation to order (s.68(2) EPCA). **You must get your evidence ready before the**

143

hearing in order to press for a good sum. You will need your estimations of your loss (see page 61), possibly revised in the light of evidence that has come up at the hearing, plus a list of all the jobs you've tried to get since you were sacked. You may also need to state the weekly amount of social security benefits you receive.

Mitigation of loss

It's up to your boss to prove that you haven't done enough to get another job, and that compensation should be reduced as a result (s.74(4) EPCA). Your boss's representative or the tribunal may want to hear your evidence about what jobs you have looked for. You will be asked to return to the witness table. Give everyone a list of the jobs you've enquired about or applied for or had interviews for. Also inform them of where you've looked for work, eg newspapers every day, Job Centre twice a week, through friends, etc.

You do not need to take the first job offered if it is not suitable. Whether a job is suitable depends on pay, status, type of work, etc. (see page 69).

The tribunal will decide whether you have taken 'reasonable' steps to get another job, or unreasonably refused an offer of reinstatement in your old job. If you have failed to "mitigate your loss", then a percentage of the compensation will be deducted. Or they may decide you should have got a job by a certain date, from which time they cut off compensation.

Settlement over compensation

Sometimes the tribunal will ask both sides to discuss compensation between themselves, to see if you can agree on a figure. They will retire, or adjourn to another date, while you try to negotiate a settlement.

If this happens, give the other side a copy of how you worked out your loss. If a section 53 claim has been successful, remember to include compensation of 2 weeks gross pay. If the tribunal have said you contributed to the dismissal, or that you have not tried hard enough to get another job, then subtract a percentage from the amount you've worked out. If the tribunal haven't stated the exact percentage contribution, and the other side are assuming a high percentage, then go back to the tribunal and ask them. Remember the 2 weeks pay for your successful section 53 claim is a fixed payment – no subtraction is made from this.

The most likely point of disagreement is future loss of earnings, ie how long it will take you to get a suitable job. Be firm. Don't agree to less than you think the tribunal would order. The average future loss awarded varies from area to area (see page 66). But argue for more than the average if it will take you longer to get another job.

If you settle now, then an advantage to both you and your boss is that no benefit will be recouped (see page 66). Although the tribunal will make an award of compensation, the amount is given as an *overall* figure, so that the "loss of earnings" part cannot be distinguished. Here the DHSS/DE will not, at present, try to recoup. So you gain as you receive the full amount, rather than a portion being paid back to the DHSS/DE.

Tribunal decides compensation

If you cannot agree, the tribunal will decide compensation. Give them your estimate of your loss. Be prepared to justify your estimate of future loss. In working out the time it will take you to get another job, the IT should consider your age, fitness, skill, and local employment situation. So point out any disadvantages you have in the job-market: eg the special difficulty of finding a job when near retirement, or if you are disabled. Consider asking the local Job Centre about the number of vacancies for your sort of work in the area, and the number of people unemployed with that trade or occupation (see the model letter on page 147). Or a trade union official could give evidence on the shortages of work locally in your occupation

After hearing the arguments from both sides, the tribunal will decide the amount. They will give their reasons and the details of how they worked it out. This may also be tape recorded.

When you get the written decision, their detailed calculations should be set out in full. Check them. In 1977, tribunals awarded less than £400 in 55% of cases, between £400 and £3000 in 43% of cases, and over £3000 in 2% of cases.

When the tribunal award compensation, any social security benefits will be recouped by the DHSS/DE from your employer (see page 66). This may mean some delay before you are paid the "loss of earnings" (or "prescribed element") part of your compensation, from which money is recouped. You should get the rest of your compensation award immediately.

Declarations

As well as reinstatement, re-engagement and compensation, tribunals have the power to make *declarations;* eg on sex discrimination, race discrimination, and failure to notify redundancies under s.101 EPA. A declaration is a statement by the tribunal that the firm has been in the wrong and needs to do something to change its practice in the future.

Costs

It is after the tribunal has given its decision, either for or against you, and sorted out compensation (if any), that the question of costs could arise. Either you or your boss may want to ask for costs.

Before the hearing, your boss's representative may have tried to put you off by saying she would claim costs against you. It's likely this was only to scare you, and she won't claim costs. But now is the time, right at the end of the hearing, when she could do this. She would claim the costs of your boss's defence to your application. You don't normally need to worry about this if you've won your case.

Costs are rarely ordered by ITs against either side (rule 11 ITRP Regs). **They are only ordered if:**
1. You acted "frivolously" or "vexatiously" or "otherwise unreasonably". *Frivolous* means you have no case and are aware of that, but still carried on with a hopeless application. There has been an increase in attempts to claim costs for this reason. Any case which is obviously not viable should be withdrawn.

Vexatious means again that you know you have no case but still persist in taking your case to an IT, just to annoy and get back at your boss. But just because your case turns out to be poor does not mean there should be costs awarded against you.

Otherwise unreasonably is a recent edition to the regulations, and is not explained. However, one

<u>Model letter to Job Centre</u>

Dear

<u>re: Mary Dee, 1 West Street, Leeds 2</u>

I am representing Ms Mary Dee in respect of an application for unfair dismissal to the Industrial Tribunal.

I require some information about her employment prospects. She was previously employed as a setter. When do you consider that you will be able to place her in a suitable vacancy? How many vacancies for this job do you have on your books at present? If there are no suitable vacancies as a setter, what are her prospects of obtaining an alternative job, and what do you consider she would be able to earn in an alternative job?

I look forward to hearing from you as quickly as possible.

Yours faithfully,

example would probably be if you were warned during a pre-hearing assessment not to continue with your case. Claims for costs on this ground are likely to increase.

2. You caused the hearing to be postponed without notice and without good reason; eg a key witness failed to turn up without reason, or mistook the day. Or if you asked for an adjournment in order to produce some documentary evidence or a witness, without any good reason why you couldn't have asked before. If this happens, the Chairperson should give you the choice of adjournment plus costs, or carrying on.

An order for costs in this situation is more likely to be made against your boss. It's your applicaton, and if you don't bring along evidence in your favour that's your tough luck. But your boss is defending his action. If he does not provide vital documents, etc, so that a post-ponement is necessary for the tribunal to have the full facts, then costs could well be awarded against him. Eg, postponement is necessary because your boss doesn't bring time sheets to the hearing when he has sacked you for persistent lateness.

A reasonable request for a postponement should be granted without any question of costs. But if, for example, your boss brings up a new allegation against you at the hearing, and you need to get another witness or some documentary evidence to counter that, you could ask for costs.

After the Hearing

Introduction

Once you have received the tribunal's decision, there may be nothing further to do.

Occasionally, however, you may find something wrong with the decision when you look through it. Perhaps compensation has been worked out wrongly, or there is something you don't understand.

Or your boss may not have carried out the tribunal's decision – you have not received your compensation for example.

Or you may feel the tribunal made a completely wrong decision and you want to appeal further to the Employment Appeal Tribunal (EAT). Or you may want to ask the tribunal to review its decision.

You may want to complain about someone or something that happened at the hearing.

Or there may be some action to take separately from your application – eg an appeal about disqualification from unemployment benefit, or a civil claim against your boss.

This section covers these possibilities.

1. CHECKING THE DECISION

The written decision arrives on average about 19 days after your hearing finished. There is an example on pages 151-154. Read it through carefully. If the Chairperson recorded the decision at the end of the hearing, this written decision should be exactly what was recorded.

Can you follow the tribunal's reasoning in the written decision (even if you don't agree with it)? If not, you may have grounds for an appeal to the EAT — see page 158.

Are the details of the compensation correct? Are they the same as decided at the end of the hearing? If there seems to be a mistake write to ROIT pointing out the mistake, and asking for clarification of the amount of compensation. If there are obvious typing errors, etc, you can also ask for these to be changed.

2. ENFORCING THE DECISION

What happens if your boss does not carry out the tribunal's decision? First contact your boss to find out what is happening — do this either directly or through ACAS.

Reinstatement And Re-engagement

Partial failure to follow the decision

Suppose the IT has made an order for reinstatement or re-engagement. **If the exact terms of the decision are not followed, the tribunal should award you extra compensation** for the loss you are caused by his failure. If your reinstatement is not complete, for example your job is not exactly as it was, or you have lost some benefits you should have, you should claim compensation. The amount is your loss from the failure to reinstate or re-engage you completely; eg from re-employing you at a later date, or at a lower rate of pay, than the tribunal ordered. The maximum compensation (the "additional award", see below) is fifty two weeks pay. See s.71 EPCA.

To claim, write to ROIT, giving the decision details,

THE INDUSTRIAL TRIBUNALS

BETWEEN

Applicant / ~~Appellant~~

Mr Laurie Malton

AND

Respondent

Rekker (Autobody Services) Ltd

DECISION OF THE INDUSTRIAL TRIBUNAL

HELD AT   Manchester   **ON**   30 January 1980

CHAIRMAN: Mr C Collins   **MEMBERS**:   Ms R Clegg
                                                    Mr J W Williams

DECISION

The unanimous/~~majority~~ decision of the Tribunal is that   the applicant was unfairly
dismissed and we award him compensation of £1,112.50.

REASONS

1. This is an application by Mr Laurie Malton born on 10 October 1942 who
complains that he was unfairly dismissed. Dismissal was admitted. The
respondents contended that they were entitled to do so by reason of redundancy.

2. We find the facts to be as follows: The applicant was employed by the
respondents as a panel beater from 26 October 1965 till 22 September 1979.
During the last 4 years of his employment he was the only full time panel
beater employed by the respondents.

3. In about 1976 the respondent's business of a car repairer had been up for
sale but at that time the negotiations were not successful. Before Christmas
1978 there had been talk about the business being sold. In April 1979 the
applicant read in the Evening News an advertisment for the sale of the
business. The respondents received several replies. About two weeks later
Mr G Rekker, the respondent's Managing Director, informed the applicant
that he could be made redundant due to the sale of the business.

4. The respondents then entered into negotiations for the sale of the business
to a Mr Campbell. The actual garage premises themselves are owned by Mr Rekker.
Mr Campbell offered the sum of £44,000. The respondents did not accept this
offer. In June 1979 the respondents received a letter from a firm of
solicitors acting on behalf of Thorpe (Salford) Ltd pointing out that their
clients had a right of pre-emption over the garage property and including
details of this Agreement. The respondents did not reply to this letter.
On 23 August 1979 Mr Campbell wrote again to the respondents informing them
that he was unable to increase his offer and asked them for their decision
in due course. Mr Rekker told the tribunal that he spoke to Mr Campbell 3
weeks later informing him that they could not agree figures. He had never
told Mr Campbell about the right of pre-emption in favour of Thorpe (Salford)
Ltd.

IT 59(TB 59)

404 527407 30M 3/77 HGW /52

5. In June 1979 the respondents informed ACAS that they were going into voluntary liquidation and that they were going to dispose of the premises and that Mr Campbell the prospective purchaser would not take on any long serving employees. They asked if it was in order for them to serve notice of redundancy on the applicant as the company was going into liquidation. They were told that it was in order for them to do so. On 30 June 1979 the applicant was given 12 weeks notice terminating his employment the reason given being: "due to the winding up of the above Company". At that time the respondents employed, in addition to the applicant, an apprentice panel beater and a cellulose sprayer. In July the appropriate redundancy forms were drafted for all 3 employees. It was the respondents' intention to dismiss the other 2 and pay them their redundancy payments. When the applicant was handed his written notice by Mr Rekker, the latter said to him, "it might go through, but if it does not you might be kept on".

6. On 7 August 1979 the respondents engaged another panel beater Mr C Ronan. He was informed that it would only be a short term employment, possibly only a fortnight. Mr Ronan is still working for the respondents. Mr Ronan and the applicant are both qualified panel beaters and were doing the same type of work.

7. The applicant was off work the week commencing 7 August and when he returned on 14 August he found the respondents had engaged Mr Ronan. They worked together in the same shop doing the same kind of work. There was sufficient work for both of them. The applicant did not approach Mr Rekker to find out why they had engaged Mr Ronan. In any event, when he was given his notice, Mr Rekker had told him that he might be kept on if the deal did not go through. He told the tribunal that if Mr Rekker had asked him during the period of his notice to stay on he would have done so. He last worked for the respondents on 22 September 1979 and received a redundancy payment of £682.50. He is still out of work and has been in receipt of unemplyment benefit.

8. Mrs Reed of the Citizens Advice Bureau who appeared for the applicant submitted that on the evedence the reason for the dismissal could not be redundancy as it was not a redundancy situation when the applicant was given his notice but just a mere possibility. Notice was premature. The respondents' business was still in fact in existence. She asked, "was it reasonable to dismiss the applicant and retain Mr Ronan?".

9. On this evidence we find that the applicant was dismissed on 22 September 1979. The first question we have to ask is whether the respondents have shown that the reason for dismissal related to redundancy. Redundancy is defined in Section 81(2) of the Employment Protection (Consolidation) Act 1978. This reads:
   "For the purposes of this Act an employeee who is dismissed shall
   be taken to be dismissed by reason of redundancy if the dismissal
   is attributable wholly or mainly to: -
       (a) the fact that his employer has ceased, or intends to cease,
       to carry on the business for the purposes of which the
       employee was employed by him, or has ceased, or intends to
       cease, to carry on that business in the place where the
       employee was so employed".
We find on the evidence and are satisfied that it was the respondents' intention to cease to carry on business as car repairers when they gave the applicant notice. It had been their intention to dispose of the business to Mr Campbell, who was to form his own Company and did not wish to employ the applicant as he was a long serving employee of the respondents, and this could have made him liable in the future should a redundancy situation have arisen to have counted the applicant's previous service with the respondents and this he was not prepared to do. After the sale of the business had been completed it was the respondents intention to liquidate the Company. We therefore find that the reason for dismissal related to redundancy.

10. The final question we have to ask ourselves is whether we are satisfied that in the circumstances having regard to fairness and common sense and the substantial merits of the case, the respondents acted reasonably in treating the redundancy as a sufficient reason for dismissing the applicant. When the respondents gave notice to the applicant terminating his employment, according to Mr Rekker the state of negotiations with Mr Campbell for the sale of the business and property were barely off the ground. There was, in addition, another fly in the ointment because Mr Rekker was not in a position to dispose of the premises to Mr Campbell because of the right of pre-emption in favour of Thorpe (Salford) Ltd. It is quite apparent to us that ACAS were not put fully in the picture and were not advised of the state of the negotiations with Mr Campbell and of the difficulty arising out of the right of pre-emption. Indeed the negotiations with Mr Campbell did not come to fruition and these negotiations have not been conducted with Mr Campbell since August last, or indeed with anyone else. Although Mr Ronan was employed on a temporary basis, he is still in the respondents' employment and there is work for him. When the 22 September arrived the respondents were no further on with the sale of their business. We find that they should at that stage have offered the applicant to retain his services and explained the position to him. If this had been done Section 2(3) of the Act would have come into operation. Had they done so we are satisfied that he would have accepted continued employment and at that stage they could have dispensed with the services of Mr Ronan if this was considered necessary, and the applicant would still be in their employment. Quite obviously they did not take into account, as they should have done, the fact that the applicant was a long serving employee of nearly 14 years standing and as Mr Ronan had only been engaged on a temporary basis no harm would have been done if he had been dismissed in place of the applicant. We were not impressed by the evidence of Mr and Mrs Rekker, who contradicted themselves and each other. We prefer the evidence of the applicant. We therefore find that the respondents did not act reasonably in treating the redundancy situation as a sufficient reason for dismissing the applicant and it follows that he was unfairly dismissed.

11. The applicant did not wish the tribunal consider reinstatement or reengagement. For the purposes of assessing compensation the following facts were agreed: — The applicant was aged 36 at the date of dismissal. His gross weekly pay was £52.50 (£45 per week net). There were no pension scheme arrangements and he had received a redundancy payment of £682.50.

12. The applicant has sought employment, so far unsuccessfully. He did not know how long it would take to find new employment. Mrs Reed on his behalf thought it would take about 3 months. We think that 6 weeks is a reasonable period to allow the applicant to obtain employment. We assess compensation as follows: —

A BASIC AWARD

13 weeks at £52.50	£682.50
Less redundancy payment received	£682.50
	Nil

B COMPENSATORY AWARD

(i) Loss of earnings from 22/9/79 to 30/1/80: 18½ weeks at £45.00 a week	£832.50
(ii) Future loss: 6 weeks at £45 a week	£270.00
(iii) Loss of statutory rights	£10.00
Total:	£1,112.50

We accordingly award him compensation of £1,112.50.

13. The following particulars are given pursuant to the Employment Protection (Recoupment of Unemployment Benefit and Supplementary Benefit) Regulations 1977.
(a) Monetary award: £1,112.50.
(b) Prescribed element: £832.50.
(c) Excess of (a) over (b): £280.00.

The applicant may not be entitled to the whole monetary award. Only (c) is payable forthwith. (b) is the amount awarded for loss of earnings without any allowance for unemployment benefit or supplementary benefit received by the applicant in respect of that period. (b) is not payable until the Department of Employment has served a notice (called a recoupment notice) on the respondents to pay the whole or a part of (b) to the Department or informs the respondents in writing that no such notice will be served. The sum named in the recoupment notice, which will not exceed (b), will be payable to the Department. The balance of (b), or the whole of it if notice is given that no recoupment notice will be served, is then payable to the applicant.

Christopher Collins
Chairman

154

and explaining how the decision has not been carried out. A new hearing will be arranged to decide the amount of compensation you should get.

If you are a trade union member, you should raise the matter through your union first — perhaps your boss has not fully understood the meaning of reinstatement or re-engagement.

Refusal to follow the decision

If your boss refuses to follow the tribunal's order at all, the IT must order your boss to give you compensation instead. Write to ROIT as above. The compensation is made up of the normal amount for unfair dismissal PLUS the "additional award" because the decision has been ignored. The amount of the additional award is decided by the tribunal, but (unless your boss satisfies them it was impossible to follow the tribunal's order) must be between 13 and 26 weeks gross pay (or between 26 and 52 weeks pay for dismissal because of sex or race discrimination or trade union activity).

The exception, where your boss proves it was impracticable to follow the tribunal's order, is very rare — it would only come up where, for example, the factory burns down.

Compensation

Suppose the IT has made a decision awarding you compensation and your boss does not pay up.

You should give him 2 weeks after you receive the decision in which to pay. If you don't hear anything in this time, phone and then write to your boss asking if he is going to pay. (Of course, if he is planning an appeal to the EAT, he does not have to pay until either the appeal is disposed of, or the time limit (6 weeks) for appealing passes and he hasn't appealed). **If he does not pay, you will have to go to the County Court (awards under £2,000), or to the High Court (awards over £2,000) to enforce the tribunal's decision.**

The county court

It may help to get advice (see page 22) if you need to go to the County Court. We give the procedure briefly. First, write to your boss again, referring to the decision and making it clear that if he doesn't pay immediately you will make a civil claim. KEEP A COPY. Give him 10 days to pay up.

If this does not produce the money, start an action in the County Court for the area where your boss's business is, claiming both the compensation and any court fees. Make sure first that 6 weeks have passed since the tribunal's decision, so that your boss has had time to appeal to the EAT. You will need to swear an "affidavit" (a statement on oath of what has happened) at the Court and leave a certified copy of the tribunal's decision and the second letter to your boss.

There will not be a hearing. The Court's order in your favour will be a formality. If your boss does not obey the Court's order, get advice from the Court.

The high court　　If the compensation awarded to you was over £2,000, you will need to sue your boss in the High Court. Get legal advice about this, from a law centre or solicitor (see page 22).

3. REVIEW OF THE TRIBUNAL'S DECISION

Grounds For Review

An IT can review (reconsider) its decision in certain circumstances (rule 10 ITRP Regs). **You can ask for a review if:**

1. There was an error by tribunal staff which led to a wrong decision (this means ROIT and COIT staff, not tribunal members). For example, you were not sent documents that you should have been, or the ROIT staff wrongly told one of your party when she arrived for the hearing that the case was not to be heard that day.

2. You (or your named representative) were not told when the hearing was to take place. You would need a good argument to persuade the tribunal that you did not receive notice, if the letter was actually posted to you.

3. The decision was made in the absence of you, your representative, or a witness. You will need a good reason why the person did not turn up to the hearing.

4. New evidence is available, since the decision was made, whose existence could not have been reasonably known or foreseen. See the note below.

5. The interests of justice require a review. This is not such a broad ground as might appear — you will not get a review, for example, just because you are unhappy with the decision. FLINT v EASTERN ELECTRICITY BOARD (1975)ITR 152: CA says review on this ground should be unusual.

6. You cannot understand how the IT worked out the compensation they have awarded you.

Note on
"new evidence"

You have to show that the new evidence was unknown or unobtainable before the hearing, would have had an important effect at the hearing, and that it is believable (though it need not be totally watertight). See LADD v MARSHALL (1954) 3 ALLER 745. If it turns out later that a witness for the other side lied at the hearing, your case for a review on the ground of new evidence (that the witness lied) would be weak unless you had cross-examined the witness at the hearing. "Important effect" means that the new evidence must be about the dismissal itself, and not, for example, about your future loss of earnings. So this ground is quite limited.

A good example of new evidence would be if a witness was unobtainable before the hearing, and afterwards was found to be able to give important evidence. It would also help your case if you could show that your employer had misdirected your search for evidence (through the further particulars procedure).

How To Ask
For A Review

You have *only 14 days* to ask for a review from the date the tribunal's decision was sent out. You could also ask at the hearing itself, but it is usually better to consider your case properly and ask after you have received the decision. the tribunal can extend this time limit, but you will need a very good reason for them to do so.

You must ask in writing for a review. Write to ROIT, giving your grounds in full. The Chairperson will first consider your request for the review, and has the power

157

to refuse it. If it goes to a tribunal hearing, the tribunal will decide what to do — either change its decision or have a completely new hearing. If it decides on a rehearing, the procedure is just the same as for the original one. This means anything you want to bring up again at the new hearing, you can (and so can your boss): you are not limited to the part of your case which led to your request for a review.

4. APPEAL TO THE EMPLOYMENT APPEAL TRIBUNAL

Right To Appeal **You have the right to appeal to the Employment Appeal Tribunal on a point of law only.** In contrast to the IT hearing, here legal aid for representation *is* available. Get advice on your appeal from a law centre, trade union, or solicitor experienced in the field. Your employer has the same right (s.136(1) EPCA). **This means you have to show one of three things:**
1. The IT did not follow the law, or misunderstood the law, or used the law wrongly.
2. The IT did not understand the major facts, or used them wrongly.
3. There was no evidence to justify the tribunal's decision. This is a decision which no reasonable tribunal could reach on the facts before it. If you are saying the tribunal or the way the hearing was carried out was biased, you must give full details in your grounds of appeal.

For a better idea of what is involved, it is useful to browse through a few EAT decisions in IRLR, to see how these points come up.

"Misunderstanding the major facts" (ground 2) does not mean simply not believing your evidence and accepting your boss's version. You must be able to show that the tribunal did not interpret the facts correctly when making its decision — for example, it based its decision on a fact that did not exist.

This right to appeal is not only about the tribunal's decision: you could also appeal about some point in the proceedings where the tribunal had made an error in law – to do with a witness order, request for further particulars, etc.

The EAT has a High Court judge who acts as Chairperson, and sits with two other members from panels of workers and employers. About 4% of unfair dismissal applications go on to the EAT.

How To Appeal   You must send your appeal in writing to arrive within 42 days of the date the tribunal's decision (or order) was sent to you. You must appeal on a special form (or use basically the same wording as the form), which you can get from the Registrar to the EAT, 4 St James' Square, London SW1 (tel 01–214 6289). Your completed appeal form should also be sent to this address, along with a copy of the decision or order which you are appealing against.

The Registrar will look at your grounds for appeal, and decide if the EAT should hear your case. If he thinks you do not have grounds for appeal, you are given a chance to send in new or altered grounds. You have a further 28 days, or whatever time of the original 42 days is left, whichever is the longer, in which to alter your appeal.

So if your boss appeals to the EAT, it could be up to 3 months after the decision before you know he is appealing (42 + 28 days).

Sometimes the EAT may have a preliminary hearing to decide if your appeal should go ahead – if your grounds really do show an arguable point of law. If the EAT decides you do not have grounds of appeal, your appeal stops there.

If it goes ahead your boss is informed, and is given a period (usually 14 days) in which to reply. Note that it is possible for your boss to "cross appeal" – he can decide to appeal himself about something he does not agree with.

There is a period before the EAT hearing when the Registrar or EAT can sort out things like whether or not some new evidence should be allowed, witnesses ordered to attend, where and when the hearing should be, etc.

159

The Hearing   Appeals to the EAT are usually heard in London and Glasgow. You can represent yourself at the hearing (although this is rare), or have a representative. Your boss will almost always have a lawyer to represent him. Because the appeal is on points of law which are often complex you should get representation, either from your trade union, a solicitor (try and find an experienced one in your area), or another experienced person (see page 22). Remember, legal aid is available.

The EAT can decide:

1. To allow your appeal. This wipes out the IT's decision. The EAT can then either give its own decision, or send your original application back to the same or another IT for a new hearing.
2. To reject your appeal.
3. To return the decision to the IT. Sometimes this will be for the IT to decide the case again in the light of the EAT's legal clarification. Sometimes it will be to ask the tribunal to explain the decision more fully. When the EAT gets the explanation it will decide according to 1. or 2. above.

Expenses of attending the EAT hearing are *not* given, except to witnesses ordered to attend.

Costs will not normally be given against you if you lose your appeal. But they can be awarded if the EAT decides the appeal was unnecessary, improper or vexatious, or where there has been unreasonable delay or conduct in bringing the appeal (rule 21, EAT rules 1976).

Higher Appeals   You can appeal from an EAT decision, on a point of law, with permission, to the Court of Appeal, and with further permission to the House of Lords. You need advice from a law centre, trade union, or solicitor experienced in employment law if you are considering this.

5. COMPLAINTS

You may have a complaint about something that has happened at or before the tribunal hearing. Perhaps a witness for the other side was allowed to read from notes while giving evidence, or the ACAS officer passed on to your boss something you had said "in confidence". Your complaint will be weakened if you have not made it clear at the time. Any complaint about a *major* point of procedure (the points above are relatively minor) could be used to get a review, or as the basis of an appeal to the EAT, instead (see pages 156 and 158). But if your complaint is about a minor point, complain as follows:

1. Complaints about COIT or ROIT staff, the lay tribunal members, or procedure at the hearing, in writing to the Secretary of the Tribunals, a regional Chairperson, or the President of the Tribunals (addresses in Appendix A).

2. Complaints about the tribunal Chairperson to the Lord Chancellor's Department (address in Appendix A).

3. Complaints about ACAS staff, in writing to ACAS head office (address in Appendix A).

6. ACTION ON OTHER FRONTS

Disqualification From Unemployment Benefit

If your were disqualified from unemployment benefit for up to 6 weeks, and appealed against the disqualification to a National Insurance Local Tribunal, your appeal may be coming up shortly (see page 116). If you won your IT case then it is likely, though not definite, you will win this appeal too: if you lost, then you still have a chance as different laws are involved. Consider advice from your trade union, an advice centre, law centre, or Tribunal Assistance Unit/Tribunal Representation Unit, or look at our companion handbook "Social Security Appeals" (Appendix B, no.8).

Civil Claim   You may have a case coming up in the County Court in which you are suing your boss for damages for breach of contract, wrongful dismissal, or another claim. Consult your solicitor or other adviser over this. See page 182.

**Redundancy –
Introduction**

Being made redundant is to be dismissed. So much of the information in this handbook about taking an unfair dismissal case to an IT can apply to redundancy. But redundancy also involves particular laws and circumstances which we deal with seperately here.

Redundancy is a "substantial reason" for dismissal (see page 39). To prove you were fairly dismissed for redundancy, your boss first has to show the redundancy is genuine: if he does this, he has jumped the "first hurdle" involved in defending your claim. But he has still to jump the second hurdle, as your dismissal for redundancy will be unfair if it is carried out unreasonably. This means not selecting you properly, failing to look for alternative jobs for you, or generally handling the redundancy in an unreasonable way.

If you believe that the redundancy is not genuine, or that it has been carried out unreasonably, then claim unfair dismissal. If the redundancy is genuine, but you

don't receive the redundancy payment you believe you are entitled to, then apply to the IT for a redundancy payment. (If you are claiming unfair dismissal, consider claiming a redundancy payment too, if you haven't already received it: if you lose the unfair dismissal claim you could still be entitled to the redundancy payment. If you win the unfair dismissal claim, note that you won't get the redundancy payment on top though, – it becomes part of your unfair dismissal compensation).

'I know it's a bit rough being made REDUNDANT by a computer, on the other hand, if anyone thinks they can handle 3,568,678 calculations per second we can still offer them a job'.

What follows are sections on redundancy situations, important in "first hurdle" disputes; on redundancy payments; and on unfair redundancy, concerning "second hurdle" disputes.

Checklist of redundancy rights

If you are redundant you are entitled to some or all of these rights:
1. Time off with pay for retraining or to seek new work.
2. Notice, or wages in lieu of notice.
3. A tax repayment if you are out of work.
4. Written reasons for your dismissal (also see page 55)
5. A redundancy payment and a statement of how it is calculated (see page 169).
6. Compensation or your job back if you have been made redundant unfairly (see page 174).

7. A "protective award" if your boss has not consulted the union (see page 178).

8. A guarantee of some debts owed to you if your employer goes bust (see page 179).

Remember, though, the best way to prevent redundancies is through collective action with your workmates — see page 8).

1. REDUNDANCY SITUATION

Redundancy involves your job NO LONGER EXISTING at the place where you were employed. This is called a "redundancy situation". There are 3 common redundancy situations:

1. Your boss's business closes or is taken over.
2. Your boss's business moves elsewhere.
3. Your boss's business has more workers than it needs.

In deciding whether you dispute anything to do with your redundancy, you first need to be clear about what is a genuine redundancy situation.

Your firm closes

Your firm is taken over

1. If your firm closes down, the redundancy situation is usually obvious. But there is also a redundancy situation if the firm closes temporarily (eg for repairs), even if you are laid off or put on short time rather than sacked. There is a complicated procedure for claiming a redundancy payment here — see s.88,89 EPCA. And there is also a redundancy situation if you are sacked when your firm *intends* to close, but has not actually done so yet. (See s.81(2)EPCA).

If the firm is taken over or changes hands, things may be more complicated (see s.94EPCA). It is a redundancy situation if your boss sacks you before the takeover or if the new owner sacks you immediately afterwards. If you are kept on, and the business is transferred as a *going concern* (same product, customers, trade name, etc), you keep continuity of

165

'He wants to know about his redundancy money'

employment and don't get a redundancy payment. But if you are kept on, eg to work the same machines but for an entirely different product, this could be transfer of just the *assets* of the old business; you should claim a redundancy payment from your old boss. If you are unsure, get a written assurance from your new boss that you will be treated as having no break in your continuity of employment. If you can't get it, claim a redundancy payment from your old boss.

Your firm moves

2. If your firm moves to a new place, there is the possibility of redundancies. It could be important whether your contract requires you to work elsewhere. If it doesn't and you don't wish to move:

* you can apply for voluntary redundancy, or failing this,

* you can resign, or you may be dismissed for unwillingness to move.

In all cases, you are redundant under s.81(2)(a) or(b), EPCA.

If your contract *does* require you to work elsewhere and you don't wish to, BEWARE:

* if you leave or resign, there is no dismissal and so no redundancy.

* if you are sacked for breach of contract, there is no redundancy (see SUTCLIFFE v HAWKER SIDDELEY LTD (1973)ICR 560: NIRC).

However, there's no duty for you to move your home — eg from London to Leeds — unless there is an express term in your contract to say so. Normally, a reasonable move would be one where you can continue to live where you are.

Even if your contract requires you to move, you could still be made redundant if less workforce is needed. Try to ensure this is genuine.

Surplus workers

3. Whether or not your firm has surplus workers is the most complicated redundancy situation. The important words (s.81(2)(b)EPCA) are whether "the requirements of the business for employees to carry out work of a particular kind ..... have ceased or diminished". We look at some possibilities below:

* If new technology means less workers or workers with different skills are needed this is normally a redundancy situation. Exceptions are if your contract requires you to work the new machines; or if you could adapt to the new methods.

'Look, I don't want those redundancies any more than you do, but we've ALL got to face the fact of a world recession'

* If the firm is overstaffed and sacks workers, there is normally a redundancy situation.
* If there is a trade recession or other cause for reducing work and your boss wishes to cut hours and wages, and you refuse and are dismissed, there is a redundancy situtation unless your contract allows your boss to impose cuts.
* If unqualified workers are sacked and replaced by qualified ones, they are *not* redundant (because the work carried out remains the same). But claim unfair dismissal if you are capable of doing the job.

* If your firm expands one side of its business but runs down another, you may be sacked for redundancy. This should not happen if your contract requires you to transfer to new work, or if the change in work is not great and you could work there.

* If your boss expects there to be a surplus and sacks you it is a redundancy situation. If he only expects the surplus to be temporary and lays you off, it is still a redundancy situation unless your contract allows him to lay you off.

* If there is a business reorganisation where you are given worse terms or conditions (eg paid less) and, for example, are sacked for refusing to accept this, there is no redundancy situation *so long as* the same number of workers are required to do the same overall amount of work. See LESNEY PRODUCTS v NOLAN (1977)IRLR 77:CA. The "kind of work" you do isn't defined by matters like hours or wages, but what you actually do. Note that there is no redundancy situation unless the *overall* requirments of the business change: duties can be swapped around among the workers so long as the overall needs are unchanged. Consider claiming unfair dismissal in this situation.

* If your contract limits you narrowly to a particular type of work and that work comes to an end, then there is a redundancy situation. However, if your contract has a wide definition of duties, and the job you are actually doing comes to an end but other work within the contract is available, there is no redundancy situation. (If you are dismissed here, your boss may argue that the main reason is not redundancy but refusing a reasonable order to transfer jobs).

Genuine redundancy

If you are made redundant, check that your job no longer exists. For example, is your job being done by someone else? Has your job, or other jobs you could have done, been advertised? If you have reason to believe the redundancy is not genuine, then claim unfair dismissal (see page 173).

2. REDUNDANCY PAY

To qualify for redundancy pay in a redundancy situation you have to fit in with 3 things:
1. You must have been dismissed for redundancy.
2. You must be eligible to apply.
3. You must not fall into one of the categories where your boss need not pay.
We deal with these in turn.

Dismissed For Redundancy?

"Dismissal" is defined in the same way as for unfair dismissal, and includes constructive dismissal — see page 33. Workers who VOLUNTEER for redundancy also count as being dismissed. If your boss disputes that you were dismissed, then it is up to YOU to prove that you were.

To qualify for a redundancy payment, the main or only reason for your dismissal must be redundancy. In redundancy payment claims it is up to YOUR BOSS to try and prove the main reason for dismissal was not redundancy but some other substantial reason, eg misconduct, incapability (see page 39) if there is any dispute over the reason for dismissal.

If there is more than one reason for dismissal, it is still up to your boss to show that redundancy was not the main reason. If a replacement has not been taken on to do your job, this will be very strong evidence towards a redundancy dismissal.

Sickness

If your firm closes down while you are off sick then this will normally be a dismissal for redundancy. Even if you are dismissed for sickness here, an IT might well find this just an excuse to avoid paying a redundancy payment.

If you are sacked when surplus to requirements when sick it is more complicated. A good pointer is if the firm has replaced you while you were sick — if not, then it is more likely an IT will decide you were sacked for redundancy.

Eligible For A Redundancy Payment?

See Table 1, page 9, for the eligibility conditions for redundancy payments. Note particularly that you must have been continuously employed for 2 years before the "relevant date" to claim a redundancy payment. The "relevant date" is almost the same as the "effective date of termination" (see page ii), except that if you are sacked without notice, the relevant date is the date when your minimum *statutory* notice would have expired (s.90(3)EPCA).

Now we go on to the special categories to look out for:

Offers Of New Work

Your boss need not pay you a redundancy payment if you unreasonably refuse an offer of a suitable alternative job (s.82EPCA). Or if you are offered your own job again — eg if a take-over firm offers to keep on existing workers, or trade picks up again and the firm withdraws its redundancy notice — and unreasonably refuse it. Any new work must be offered before you finish your present job.

If your own job is offered back to you, it would probably only be reasonable to refuse it if you were offered it at the last minute, and had already fixed up another job; or if there was no prospect of your job extension being more than very temporary.

Any alternative job must be offered before your old contract ends. and must start within 4 weeks. The work must be suitable, and you can try it out for a month

'When you said the job involved a new approach to selling I don't think you gave me a clear idea of the WORKING CONDITIONS'

170

without prejudicing your redundancy payment right. It is up to YOUR BOSS to prove that he offered suitable employment and that you refused it unreasonably. Most disputes over alternative employment centre round "suitability" and "reasonableness".

Suitability

Suitable means "substantially equivalent" — so it means more than just, say, the same pay. The main factors to consider are pay, hours, skills required, any change of status, physical demands, how long the job is expected to last, any increased travelling to work, and whether you need to move home. So a Class 1 HGV driver offered a job as a Class 2 driver; a lorry driver offered labouring work; and a manager offered a job as a sales representative were all found to have been offered unsuitable jobs.

Reasonableness

If the new employment *is* suitable and you do not try it out for at least some of the trial period, it will often be unreasonable to refuse it. Reasonableness depends on domestic circumstances, travel time and expense, effect on health, lack of job security, last minute offers, and other personal reasons. There is some overlap with suitabilitiy, but reasonableness concerns more personal factors to do with the job. So a worker with arthritis who feared she couldn't cope with the new job; and a worker who had a serious disagreement with her future boss and thought the new job couldn't last long both refused the new offers reasonably.

Misconduct

If you are dismissed for redundancy, but could have been dismissed for misconduct, s.82(2)EPCA gives your boss an escape from paying redundancy money. Employers escape having to pay if they were entitled to sack you on the spot for misconduct. So they have to prove that gross misconduct took place (see page 41).

There is a very complicated situation if you are under notice of dismissal for redundancy and then are dismissed for misconduct (so you are sacked twice). Basically, s.82(2) combined wth s.92EPCA mean that your redundancy payment award may be *reduced* in these circumstances, rather than wiped out altogether.

The IT decides by how much the payment should be reduced.

Strikes

Strikes sometimes lead to a business closing; often where the business is on the verge of collapse anyway. Here the argument is whether the dismissal is for redundancy or because of the strike. It is often difficult to show the dismissal was mainly for redundancy – one example could be if the strike was only a reaction to the redundancy situation. Even where the strike *is* only a secondary reason, s.82(2)EPCA (see above) may lead to loss of the redundancy payment, as the EAT have decided that striking is conduct which justifies instant dismissal. (But if some workers are taken back, claim unfair dismissal – see page 44).

Claiming A Redundancy Payment

Write to your employer to claim a redundancy payment within 6 months of becoming redundant. If you have worked for a trial period at an alternative job, the 6 months runs from the date your trial period ended. Once you have sent in your claim there is no time limit for actually applying to the IT to decide your case.

Alternatively, if you think your boss is unlikely to pay, claim on form IT1 within the same 6 month time limit.

Late claim

There is a 6 month extension of the time limit (s.101(2) EPCA) where it is "just and equitable" to allow this, which an IT could grant. Examples could be if you had been told by your boss that you would be given a redundancy payment but were not; or were misled by ACAS advice; or were ignorant of your right to claim.

Amount of redundancy payment

The redundancy payment is calculated in exactly the same way as the basic award for unfair dismissal – see page 62. Note that there cannot be any reduction of the award here though; contributory fault applies only to unfair dismissal. The maximum redundancy payment is at present £3,900.

Will you stop going on about your REDUNDANCY MONEY

3. UNFAIR REDUNDANCY

What Is Unfair Redundancy?

This section mainly concerns cases where a redundancy situation is not disputed, but where you believe that your boss has not acted reasonably in making you redundant. This could be to do with your personal selection or not following correct procedure. Your boss not adopting any criteria for selection for redundancy or not having fully considered alternative jobs are the most common cases of unreasonable behaviour.

Here you make an unfair dismissal claim on the basis of unfair redundancy. It is possible to claim a redundancy payment as well as unfair redundancy. (see page 163).

Unfair selection for redundancy

Your selection for redundancy is unfair (s.59(b) EPCA) **if:**

1. You were chosen because of trade union membership or activities, or for refusing to join a closed shop on conscience grounds. It is up to YOU to prove this.

2. Your selection was a departure from an agreed procedure or customary arrangement without there being any special reason for this departure. It is up to YOU to prove that there is a customary or agreed procedure and that there has been a departure from it.

To claim, there must be at least one other worker in the same job who has been kept on, who you can compare yourself with.

Your boss may not have adopted any criteria for selection at all. But "last in, first out" is not the only reasonable selection procedure — your boss can use any other test as so long as it is reasonable. He will be expected to explain his criteria to the IT. It is not enough to show that another method of selection would also be reasonable — nor is it that the tribunal themselves would have used a different method. In effect, you would have to show that no reasonable employer would have acted in that way (see WATLING & CO LTD v RICHARDSON (1978)IRLR 255: EAT).

Offers of new work

Was there work for you in the same firm or an associated firm? Were you offered it? Paragraph 46 of the Industrial Relations Code of Practice (see Appendix B) says management should "offer help to employees in finding other work". This certainly means they should try and find you another job in the firm.

Important Points About Unfair Redundancy And Redundancy Pay

There are three important points to note about unfair redundancy claims and how they tie in with redundancy payment claims:

You can claim with less service

1. You can claim a redundancy payment only after you have worked for 2 years, but a claim for unfair redundancy can be made with less service — after 52 weeks at work. (Note: not in small firms — see page 10).

You cannot get double payment

2. You will not receive a double award of compensation for unfair redundancy and a redundancy payment if you win both claims. Any redundancy payment you get is taken off the unfair redundancy compensation, so the maximum you can get is the maximum unfair redundancy compensation.

What your boss has to prove is different

3. The question of trying to prove redundancy is completely opposite in an unfair redundancy case from a redundancy payment case. Proving unfair redundancy goes just like ordinary unfair dismissal cases; it is up to your employer to prove that you were dismissed for redundancy — a substantial reason. In a redundancy payment case, redundancy is assumed to be the reason for dismissal unless your employer proves otherwise.

In other words, in resisting a redundancy payment case your boss will probably be saying "no redundancy". In resisting an unfair redundancy case, he will normally be saying "redundancy".

Claiming Unfair Redundancy

Generally, claiming unfair redundancy is difficult to succeed in. Proving there is a redundancy situation and that this is the main reason for dismissal is usually not difficult. The tribunal will not look at the firm's wisdom in closing the business or saying they no longer need you, for example, so long as it is a genuine redundancy situation.

Even if your boss cannot prove redundancy, this does not mean your dismissal will be unfair. Where you were sacked in a re-organisation "designed to improve performance and efficiency", the IT will often accept the sacking as for "some other substantial reason" (see page 43 and WILSON v UNDERHILL HOUSE SCHOOL (1977)IRLR 475: EAT).

Examples of Unfair Redundancy Cases

A good way of understanding how ITs are dealing with unfair redundancy is to look at some cases:

H shut down their factory and made the whole workforce redundant. M claimed compensation for unfair dismissal and challenged the validity of H's decision, maintaining that the factory could be economically viable and therefore it was "unfair" to declare redundancy.

The EAT held that they had no power to investigate the reasons for creating redundancy or the rights and wrongs of industrial disputes. There was a redundancy situation and M had been dismissed for this reason. There was no unfair redundancy (though note M could still be entitled to a redundancy payment). MOON & OTHERS v HOMEWORTHY FURNITURE (NORTHERN) LTD (1977)ICR 117:EAT.

There was a redundancy situation at D, and management decided to do away with the whole night shift, although selection by "LIFO" had been used for previous redundancies. The tribunal decided LIFO was not the customary arrangement here, and management's decision was not unreasonable. The IT "was not in a position to criticise the manner in which an employer decides its work must be cut down". So the redundancy was not unfair. GUY v DELANAIR (CAR HEATER) LTD. (1975)IRLR 73: IT.

In a redundancy situation, G had to choose which of two workers had to be made redundant. W was chosen and claimed unfair redundancy.
The QBD decided that in cases like this, where there was very little to choose between the two workers, then whichever one is chosen the dismissal would probably be fair provided the employer acted genuinely. So the redundancy was not unfair. GRUNDY (TEDDINGTON) LTD v WILLIS. (1976)ICR 323: CA.

An electrician, R, was made redundant in a redundancy situation while two other electricians on another site who had only been employed for 10 days were kept on.
The EAT decided that even if selection on a site basis was the custom of the industry, it was still unreasonable in the circumstances under s.57(3) EPCA. So the redundancy was unfair. WATLING & CO LTD v RICHARDSON. (1978)IRLR 255: EAT.

In a redundancy situation the agreed procedure for selection was that volunteers would go first. However, B refused to make one of them redundant and instead made W, not a volunteer, redundant.
The EAT decided the company had a "special reason" for not following the agreed procedure — the volunteer had 19 years experience and was needed by the company to keep business alive — so the redundancy was not unfair. WESTON v BENTLEY ENGINEERING CO LTD. (1977): EAT

176

There was a redundancy situation and K was made redundant without any warning or consultation.

The EAT decided the redundancy was unfair, as the employer had ignored both the Industrial Relations code of practice, para. 46, and s.99 of the EPA on warning and consultation.
KELLY v UPHOLSTERY & CABINET WORKS (AMESBURY) LTD. (1977)IRLR 91: EAT.

B was made redundant without any attempt being made to see if he could be employed somewhere else within the group. Also, he was not allowed any time off to look for new work.

NIRC decided his redundancy was unfair because of the failure to look for alternative work for him, and the fact that there was no effective administrative machinery to do so was no excuse.
VOKES LTD v BEAR. (1974)ICR 1: NIRC.

Later decisions have limited this decision, but it is still the case that companies must try to find other work for redundant workers, and bring evidence of this to the hearing if the worker makes this part of her complaint. And companies must not assume a worker will reject an alternative job, even if it involves demotion, without asking the worker (see AVONMOUTH CONSTRUCTION CO LTD v SHIPWAY, (1979)IRLR 14).

Further reading   IDS Supplements numbers 14–19 all cover different aspects of redundancy and insolvency in very useful detail which includes case law. See Appendix B for details.

4. CONSULTATION OVER REDUNDANCIES

Need For Consultation   **If your boss has not consulted the recognised trade union about the redundancies, the union can claim a "protective award" (s.99 EPA) on your behalf, on top of any redundancy payment or unfair redundancy award you might claim.**

Warnings to and consultation with all workers are recommended by the Industrial Relations code of practice, para. 46. And warnings and consultation are required on all redundancies under the EPA, no matter how few, unless there are special circumstances. This applies wherever a union is recognised, and covers workers who are not union members so long as the union bargains for other workers in their category.

The union must be consulted in writing, and given information on matters like reasons for the redundancies, numbers involved, method of selection, and over what period the redundancies are to be carried out.

The special circumstances in which firms need not consult are normally limited to financial emergency, such as an order winding up the company, or unexpected cuts in vital orders.

Period for consultation

Firms must give a minimum period for consultation before the redundancies happen. The more workers are due for redundancy, the longer the consultation period required:
* If more than 100 workers are to be made redundant, over a period of 90 days or less, consultation must begin *at least* 90 days before anyone is dismissed.
* If between 10 and 100 workers are to be made redundant, over a period of 30 days or less, consultation must begin *at least* 30 days before anyone is dismissed.
* If less than 10 workers are to be made redundant, a guideline to the length of consultation required is 28 days (see EEPTU v VAN GARVEY ELECTRICAL LTD).

The Protective Award

If the firm does not consult properly, the union can claim a protective award and go to an Industrial Tribunal. This award is one of so many days pay for the workers affected. IT's decide how long the period the award covers should be on the basis of how serious the firm's failure to consult is, but it cannot be more than the minimum consultation period.

So the maximum period the award covers is 90, 30 or 28 days, depending on the number of workers affected and over what period they are made redundant (see above).

No right to a protective award

You are disqualified from receiving any form of protective award in various circumstances:
* If you are on strike, or suspended without pay, during

178

the period covered by the protective award (s.102(4) EPA).

* If you are sacked fairly for some other reason than redundancy during the period covered by the protective award (s.102(5)(a) EPA).

* If you "unreasonably resign" during the period covered by the protective award (s.102(5)(b) EPA). This certainly should not include leaving to go to another job.

* If you unreasonably refuse your old job back, or a suitable alternative job (s.102(7) EPA).

The Protective Award And Unfair Redundancy

Failure to consult the trade union can make your dismissal for redundancy unfair, where this failure makes a real difference to the situation. See BRITISH UNITED SHOE MACHINERY v CLARKE (1978) ICR 70: EAT. For example, consultation might have meant other workers would have been selected for redundancy instead of you, or you would have been able to find another job more easily. Compensation awarded by the IT is often small if the only thing unfair about your dismissal is failure to consult.

5. YOUR EMPLOYER GOES BUST

"Insolvency" is the technical word for the situation when your employer goes bust. If this happens, you have the right to get back some of the wages, holiday pay, redundancy pay, etc that your boss owes to you. There are two different courses open to you here:

Claiming Under The Companies Act

1. *Your rights under the Companies Act 1948 and the Insolvency Act 1976.* These Acts allow you to claim money owed to you as a "preferential creditor" up to a limit of £1040. This means you are paid before some shareholders out of any money that the company has left. You count as a preferential creditor for up to 4 months owed wages. "Wages" includes holiday pay, sick pay, guarantee payments, medical suspension pay, payment for time off for union duties or looking for

179

work and protective award pay. Income tax, national insurance contributions and pension scheme contributions are subtracted from the total where relevant.

I've just been reading this BOOK ABOUT INDUSTRIAL TRIBUNALS – it almost makes you glad you haven't got a job!

For any other money (eg deductions from wages for savings, wages over £1040) you have to take your chance with all the other creditors. To get the money, write to your boss's liquidator/receiver/trustee. He sends you a form to fill in depending on the type of debt.

Claiming From The Redundancy Fund

2. *Your rights under EPCA, from the Redundancy Fund.* Under EPCA (s.121 onwards) you can claim some debts (within certain limits changed each year) from the Redundancy Fund, paid to you by the Secretary of State for Employment. This course should be followed where there is not enough money to pay preferential creditors, or where you are claiming debts not covered by course 1 but covered by course 2.

The debts covered here are:

1. Up to 8 weeks arrears of wages and up to 6 weeks

180

arrears of holiday pay up to a limit of £130 a week. "Wages" includes guarantee payments, medical suspension pay, payment for time off for trade union duties or looking for work, and protective award pay.

2. Pay in lieu of statutory notice (up to £130 a week).

3. Basic award of unfair dismissal compensation, in full.

4. Apprenticeship premium.

5. Unpaid employer's contributions to pension schemes.

6. Redundancy pay (s.106 EPCA).

Your employer should give you the DE claim forms: if you have difficulty, write directly to the DE (address in Appendix A). If the DE will not pay you, you can apply to an IT.

TABLE 2   OTHER CLAIMS

1. *Breach of contract.* Your right to have all the terms of your contract followed by your boss. If he breaks them; eg does not give you enough notice, or holiday pay, or he fines you or makes illegal deductions from your wages (and your contract allows you holiday pay, or does not say he can fine you) — you can sue either for debt or for "breach of contract" in the civil court (usually the County Court). In practice you can only get a money award of damages from the court; it will not order your boss to keep you on. Remember too that if you are still employed when you sue your boss, and have worked less than 52 weeks, you will have no protection if he sacks you. County Court officers can give you some help with making your claim. Note: a serious breach of contract by your employer ends the contract if you leave as a result — you could have a case for applying to an IT for unfair dismissal (see page 34: "constructive dismissal"). The time limit for starting a breach of contract claim is 6 years from the date of the breach.

It is possible to have both a breach of contract claim and an unfair dismissal claim going on at the same time. s.131 EPCA allows for the possibility of ITs taking breach of contract cases, but at present there is no sign of this section coming into force.

2. *Wrongful dismissal.* Your right to sue for "wrongful dismissal" in the County Court. This is an extremely limited right, and is nothing to do with "unfair dismissal". In practice it is limited to cases where your boss does not give you enough notice (or pay in lieu of notice) when he sacks you, or where he fails to carry out the proper disciplinary procedure before he sacks you (GUNTON v LONDON BOROUGH OF RICHMOND (1980)IRLR 321: CA). It may also be possible to claim for loss of pension rights where your loss is greater than the maximum unfair dismissal award — you would claim the extra through Court.

The damages for wrongful dismissal are generally limited to your loss of earnings during the period of notice you were entitled to (in your contract notice or statutory notice, whichever is the greater). For ordinary workers this is not likely to be a very large amount (the maximum statutory notice is 12 weeks). For a dismissed manager on a 5 year fixed contract, however, the damages could be a large amount. The time limit for wrongful dismissal claims is 6 years from the dismissal. We suggest you see a solicitor for advice (through the Green Form scheme if possible) if you wish to bring a wrongful dismissal claim.

3. *Minimum wage.* Your right to a minimum rate for your job, if you work in one of the industries covered by Wages Councils (hotels, catering, hairdressing, the rag trade, retailing, etc). Wages Councils also cover holidays and some other conditions of employment. If you are not getting the minimum rate: DE inspectors can prosecute in a Magistrates Court — you can get arrears of wages up to 2 years; OR you can sue in the County Court for wages arrears of up to 6 years. See the DE guide "Minimum Wages" (Appendix B), or contact the relevant Wages Inspectorate (details and address from any advice centre).

4. *Your employer goes bust.* See page 179.

5. *Social security benefits.* Your right to some form of social security while you are out of work. This could be a contributory benefit such as unemployment benefit (see page 58 about 6 week disqualification from benefit for misconduct or voluntarily leaving work). Or it could be another contributory benefit such as sickness benefit or maternity allowance. Or it could be a non-contributory benefit such as disablement benefit, industrial injury benefit or supplementary benefit. An advice centre, law centre, or CPAG handbooks "Guide to Non-Means Tested Social Security Benefits" and "National Welfare Benefits Handbook" should tell you what you are entitled to. If you are refused then you generally have the right of appeal. See Appendix B for details of the above handbooks, and the companion handbooks to this one, which deal with appeal problems with these benefits.

6. *Accident at work.* If you are injured at work, claim damages from your employer if you can show he did not provide:
* safe plant and equipment.
* competent fellow workers.
* adequate supervision and instruction. OR
* a safe place of work and a safe system of work.

   Speed in claiming is very important. Get advice from your trade union, an advice centre or law centre, or a solicitor on this. Damages are given for loss of earning power; for pain and suffering; for loss of ability to enjoy hobbies and pleasures; and for actual loss of money, eg loss of wages or damage to clothing.
   Separately from any civil claim, you should also claim national insurance benefits for any incapacity or disability caused by your work. Industrial injury benefit, disablement benefit and death benefit are the possible

benefits. Claim as soon as possible — get advice if necessary. "The Hazards of Work" by Patrick Kinnersley (Pluto Press, paperback) provides very useful information on accidents at work.

7. *Conditions at work.* Improving working conditions is difficult. There are many laws, setting different standards, and few with any real teeth.

Read "Hazards of Work" (see 6. above) for information on statutory safety standards; the various factories, offices and agricultural safety Acts and how to enforce them; pollution; and general health and safety at work.

APPENDIX A — Useful Addresses

Central Office of Industrial Tribunals (COIT)	93 Ebury Bridge Road, London SW1W 8RE. tel 01–730 9161.

REGIONAL OFFICES (ROITs) of Industrial Tribunals:

Aberdeen ROIT	252 Union St., Aberdeen AB1 1TN. tel 0224 52307.
Ashford ROIT	Tufton House, Tufton Street, Ashford, Kent TN23 1RJ. tel 0233 21346.
Birmingham ROIT	Phoenix House, 1-3 Newall St., Birmingham B3 3NH. tel 021-236 6051
Bristol ROIT	43-51 Price St., Bristol BS1 4PE. tel 0272 298261.
Bury St. Edmunds ROIT	118 Northgate Street, Bury St Edmunds, Suffolk IP33 1HQ tel 0284 62171.
Cardiff ROIT	Caradog House, 1-3 St. Andrew's Place, Cardiff CF1 3BE. tel 0222 372693.
Dundee ROIT	13 Albert Square, Dundee DD1 1DD. tel 0382 21578.
Edinburgh ROIT	11 Melville Crescent, Edinburgh EH3 7LU. tel 031-226 5584.
Exeter ROIT	Renslade House, Bonhay Road, Exeter EX4 3BX. tel 0392 79665.
Leeds ROIT	Minerva House, East Parade, Leeds LS1 5JZ. tel 0532 459741.
Liverpool ROIT	1 Union Court, Cook St., Liverpool L2 4UJ. tel 051-236 9397.
London (North) ROIT	19-29 Woburn Place, London WC1. tel 01-632 4921.
London (South) ROIT	93 Ebury Bridge Road, London SW1W 8RE. tel 01-730 9161.
Manchester ROIT	Alexandra House, 14-22 The Parsonage, Manchester M3 2JA. tel 061-833 0581.
Newcastle ROIT	Watson House, Pilgrim St., Newcastle on Tyne NE1 6RB. tel 0632 28865.
Nottingham ROIT	Birkbeck House, Trinity Square, Nottingham. tel 0602 45701.
Sheffield ROIT	Fargate Court, Fargate, Sheffield S1 2HU. tel 0742 70348.
Southampton ROIT	149a High Street, Southampton. tel 0703 31236.

EMPLOYMENT APPEAL TRIBUNAL
(EAT)

4 St James's Square, London SW1. tel 01-214 6000 or
01-214 3367.

(in Scotland)　　　249 West George Street, Glasgow G2 4QE. tel 041-248 6213.

ACAS OFFICES

Head Office　　　Cleland House, Page St., London SW1P 4ND. tel 01-222 4383

Midlands Region　　　Alpha Tower, Suffolk St., Queensway, Birmingham B1 1TZ. tel 021-643 9911.

Northern Region　　　Westgate House, Westgate Road, Newcastle on Tyne NE1 1TJ tel 0632 612191.

North West Region　　　Boulton House, 17-21 Chorlton St., Manchester M1 3NY. tel 061-228 3222.

South East Region　　　Hanway House, Red Lion Square, London WC1R 4NR. tel 01-405 8454.

South West Region　　　16 Park Place, Clifton, Bristol BS8 1JP. tel 0272 211921.

Yorkshire and Humberside Region　　　City House, Leeds LS1 4JH. tel 0532 38232.

Scotland　　　109 Waterloo St., Glasgow G2 7DY. tel 041-204 2677.

Wales　　　Phase 1, Ty-Glas Road, Llanishen, Cardiff CF4 5PH. tel 0222 762636.

Department of Employment Regional Offices

Head Office　　　8 St James's Square, London SW1Y 4JR. tel 01-214 6000.

Midlands Region　　　2 Duchess Place, Hadley Road, Fiveways, Birmingham B16 8NS. tel 021-455 7111.

Northern Region　　　93a Grey St., Newcastle on Tyne NE1 6HE. tel 0632 27575.

North Western Region　　　Sunley Buildings, Picadilly Plaza, Manchester M60 7JS. tel 061-832 9111.

South Eastern Region and London Region.　　　Clifton House, 83-117 Euston Road, London NW1 2RB. tel 01-388 5100.

South Western Region　　　The Pithay, Bristol BS1 2NQ. tel 0272 291071.

Yorkshire and Humberside Region	City House, Leeds LS1 4JH. tel 0532 38232.
Scotland	43 Jeffrey St., Edinburgh EH1 1UU. tel 031-556 8433.
Wales	Companies House, Crown May, Maindy, Cardiff CF4 3UW. tel 0222 388588.
Commission for Racial Equality	Elliott House, 10-12 Allington Street, London SW1. tel 01-828 7022.
Equal Opportunities Commission	Overseas House, Quay St., Manchester M3 3HM. tel 061-833 9244.
Small Firms Information Centre.	65 Buckingham Palace Road, London SW1W 0QX. tel 01-828 2384.
Health and Safety Executive	Baynards House, 1 Chepstow Place, London W2 4TN. tel 01-229 3456.
National Association of Citizens Advice Bureaux	110 Drury Lane, London WC2. tel 01-836 9231.

APPENDIX B — Useful books, handbooks, pamphlets and reference works

1. PRACTICAL GUIDES — Books and handbooks

1 and 2, 6–8 from: any bookshop, probably by ordering.

1 also from:
Pluto Press, Unit 10 Spencer Court, 7 Chalcot Road, London NW1 8LH.

2 also from:
NCCL, 186 Kings Cross Road, London WC1 9DE

3 from:
TUC, Congress House, Gt. Russell Street, London WC1B 3LS

4 from:
LAG. 28a Highgate Road, London NW5

5 from:
LRD, 78 Blackfriars Road, London SE1 8HF.

8 also from:
NACAB Training Dept., 110 Drury Lane, London WC2.

9 from:
WEA, 9 Upper Berkeley Street, London W1H 8BY.

1. "Rights at Work" £2.95 1979, by Jeremy McMullen. Publ. Pluto Press.

Excellent summary of employment law and how to use it. Clearly written — the best basic reference book available.

2. "Your Rights at Work" 70p 1979, by Patricia Hewitt. Publ. National Council for Civil Liberties.

Briefer guide to all the individual employment rights. Clearly written; very basic.

3. TUC guides: "Redundancy", "Maternity", "Unfair Dismissal". Each 20p 1976/77, publ. TUC.

Very short; basic information only on each topic.

4. "LAG Guide to Unfair Dismissal" — due in 1981.

awaiting information

5. "Women's Rights at Work" 60p + 10p postage, 1979, publ. Labour Research Department.

Detailed guide to women's employment rights, including case law. Rather heavy reading.

6. "The Industrial Tribunals Handbook" £15 by Bowes Egan, 1978. Publ. New Commercial Publishing Company.

Step-by-step detailed procedure for taking a case to an IT, including examples. Especially useful to anyone thinking of representing at the IT hearing.

7. "Industrial Tribunals — Practice and Procedure" £15, 1980, by D Williams and D Walker. Publ. Butterworths.

An alternative to 6. above. Has more detail in some areas, but without examples and written more legally.

10 from:
NETUSIU,
'Southend',
Fernwood Road,
Newcastle on Tyne
NE2 1TJ.

11 from:
LRD, 78 Blackfriars
Road, London SE1.

8. "Social Security Appeals" — a guide to National Insurance Local Tribunals and Medical Appeal Tribunals" 1980, publ. National Association of Citizens Advice Bureaux.

Companion handbook to this one, on problems to do with social security benefits (except supplementary benefit) and appeals about them. Written with practical examples, cartoons, etc.

9. "Preparing for Industrial Tribunals" 30p + 10p postage, 1979. Publ. Workers Educational Association.

Checklist covering tactics and procedure for IT preparation and representation, Knowledge of the law is assumed.

10. "TUSUI Information Kit: Working Guides for Trade Unionists" £5 1978. Publ. North East Trade Union Studies Information Unit.

Loose leaf binder and 17 guides to employment law and trade union activity. Simply written; basic information only, will be updated. Emphasis on collective action. Useful basic information.

11. "Unfair Dismissal" 50p + 13p postage 1980. Publ. Labour Research Dept.

Brief but useful booklet on unfair dismissal.

2. PRACTICAL GUIDES — Pamphlets

Department of Employment Series on Employment Protection:

1. "Written statement of main terms and conditions of employment" (on contract of employment).
2. "Procedure for handling redundancies".
3. "Employee's rights on insolvency of employer" (when your boss goes bust).
4. "Employment rights for the expectant mother".
5. "Suspension on medical grounds under health and safety regulations".
6. "Facing redundancy? — time off for job hunting or to arrange training".
7. "Trade union membership and activities".
8. "Itemised pay statement".
9. "Guarantee payments".
10 ."Terms and conditions of employment".
11. "Rules governing continuous employment and a week's pay".

12. "Time off for public duties".
13. "Unfairly dismissed?".
14. "Rights on termination of employment".

also: "Contracts of Employment Act 1972" (a guide to the Act and how it affects individual rights)

and: "Individual Rights of Employees"

All these pamphlets are free, and can be obtained from local DE offices, regional DE offices, law centres and some advice centres. They are updated from time to time.

Codes of Practice:

"Industrial Relations Code of Practice" 15p, HMSO or government bookshops.
"ACAS Code of Practice 1: Disciplinary practice and procedures in employment" (also included in the DE guide "Individual Rights of Employees").

"ACAS Code of Practice 3: Time off for trade union duties and activities"
            both 15p from HMSO or government bookshops.
"Code of Practice: Picketing" and
"Code of Practice: Closed Shop Agreements and Arrangements" both free from DE Regional Offices.

Other pamphlets:

"Sex Discrimination — a guide to the Sex Discrimination Act 1975" free from the EOC.
"Equal Opportunities — a guide for employees" free from the EOC.
"Equal Pay — a guide to the Equal Pay Act 1970" free from the EOC.
"Guide to the Race Relations Act 1976" free from the CRE.

12 from:
NCCL
186 Kings Cross Rd.
London WC1X 9DE

13 from:
EOC
Overseas House
Quay Street
Manchester
M3 3HN

12 "Gayworkers—trade unions and the law" £1.20 1981. Publ. NCCL

13 "Sex discrimination and equal pay — How to prepare your own case for an Industrial Tribunal". Free. 1979, publ. EOC

14 "National Welfare Benefits Handbook". £1.50 Publ. CPAG. 1980/81

Excellent handbook on discrimination encountered by gay workers and present case law on unfair dismissal and gays.

A basic, but useful guide to case preparation in these areas

A very useful guide to the main non-contributory benefits.

14 & 15 from: CPAG 1 Macklin Street London WC2B 5NH	15 "Rights Guide to Non-Means Tested Social Security Benefits". £1.35 Publ. CPAG, 1980	As above, but for social security benefits – well set out and easy to follow.

3. THE LAW AND CASE LAW

16 – 18 from: law bookshops; or others by ordering.	16 "Encyclopedia of Labour Relations Law" £45 + updating charge, eds. B.Hepple and P.O'Higgins. Publ. Sweet & Maxwell.	Comprehensive (3 volume) guide to all employment law, regularly updated. Full text of all laws, + important case law.
16 &17 also from: Sweet & Maxwell, North Way, Andover Hants.	17 "The Law of Redundancy" £19.75. 1980, by C.Grunfeld. Publ. Sweet & Maxwell.	Full guide to lay-offs, redundancy, and unfair redundancy law, including important case law
19 from: The Industrial Soc., PO Box 1BQ, Robert Hyde House, 48 Bryanston Square, London W1H 1BQ	18 "Harvey on Industrial Relations and Employment Law" £38 + supplements, ed. R Harvey. Publ. Butterworths.	An alternative to 16 above. Cheaper, but slightly less easy to use and without the 'Encyclopedia's' useful comments.
20–22 from: government bookshops, or HMSO, 49 High Holborn, London WC2	19 "A guide to the Employment Protection (Consolidation) Act 1978" £1, 1978 by Joan Henderson. Publ. The Industrial Society.	Written for employers, but good value if you just want to quote from and understand this Act.
23 & 24 from: IDS, 140 Great Portland Street, London W1	20 "The Employment Protection (Consolidation) Act 1978" £3, publ. HMSO	The Act alone. 16 above would be a better buy.
	21 "Sex Discrimination Act 1975" £1.35 HMSO	
25 from: Marketing Manager IRLR, 170 Finchley Road, London NW3 6BP.	22 "Race Relations Act 1976" £1.35 HMSO.	
	23 IDS Handbooks; eg – 1 'Unfair dismissal'. 4 'The new race law and employment'. 6 'Redundancy source book'.	The handbooks cover practice on each topic through easy to follow case law. The language is simple and they are **very useful**. Advice centres should certainly consider subscribing (see below).

26 from:
LAG,
28a Highgate Road,
London NW5

12 'Unfair dismissal updated'.
14 'Equal pay, sex discrimination and maternity rights'.
15 'Handling dismissals'
16 'Going to a tribunal'.

Each £2.50 for subscribers £4.00 for non-subscribers. Publ. IDS.

24 IDS Supplements and Briefs. Examples of Supplements:—
15 'Dismissed for redundancy'.
18 'Claiming redundancy'
19 'Unfair redundancy'
21 'Constructive dismissal'
24 'Sickness dismissals'
26 'Theft and dishonesty dismissals'
28 'Capability dismissals' Subscription rates on application. Publ. IDS.

Only available to subscribers. The Supplements update and expand the handbooks (see above). The briefs come out fortnightly and keep up to date with important aspects. There is also a whole range of other publications on employment.

25 "Industrial Relations Law Reports" £48 per year (monthly).

Best of the case law journals. Contains recent cases in detail; easy to follow.

26 "LAG Bulletin" £1.65 monthly.

Keeps up to date with (amongst others) important case law and changes in employment law.

4. RESEARCH MATERIAL

27 from:
HMSO,49 High Holborn,
London WC2

27 "Employment Gazette" £23.52 per year (monthly). Publ. HMSO

Masses of facts and statistics on employment.

A

B

C

W